THE COMPANION BOOK OF

Herbs

THE COMPANION BOOK OF

Herbs

DIANA CRAIG
&
SARAH HARRIS

Oceana

An Oceana Book

This book is published by
Oceana Books
The Old Brewery
6 Blundell Street
London N7 9BH

Copyright ©1998 Quantum Books Ltd

ISBN 1-86160-215-4

OCEEOH

Project Manager: Rebecca Kingsley
Project Editor: Sarah Harris
Designer: Bruce Low

Typeset in Sabon
Manufactured in Singapore by Eray Scan Pte. Ltd
Printed in Singapore by Star Standard Industries Pte. Ltd

Contents

Introduction to Herbs

Herbs were once an essential part of people's lives, as flavourings for foods, remedies for ailments and their symptoms, and aids to beauty. Of these three usages, only the first has continued into modern times. However, disenchantment with conventional medicine and concern for the wellbeing of the planet and all the life forms on it has encouraged people to look for more natural, harmonious and less harmful ways of living, and the long-forgotten uses of herbs are once more being explored.

THE CULTURE OF HERBS

A small range of dried culinary herbs are familiar products on supermarket and grocery shelves and the broadening of popular taste brought about by increased travel means that a few of the more unusual herbs, such as basil and coriander, can now be brought fresh. Whether dried or fresh, however, the available range is still only a small percentage of all the herbs that can be grown. Growing your own plants not only increases the herbs available to you, but brings other pleasures, too.

The contrasting colours and forms of the different plants are an aesthetic pleasure in themselves and the scents of the leaves and flowers are a sensual delight, adding much to the character of any garden, patio or balcony. Many herbs are also attractive to bees so that a herb bed or collection of pots will hum will a sleepy drone all summer long.

But the least obvious – yet perhaps most important – aspect of growing your own herbs lies in what might be called the 'culture of herbs'. Useful herbs have grown wild or been cultivated for hundreds and, in some cases, thousands of years, so in growing your own you are reviving and evoking an ancient tradition. When you plant, tend, weed or water them – or just wander by them appreciating their variety

Elder flowers and berries make delicious summer drinks.

Bay.

Mint.

and fragrance – you are sharing an experience enjoyed by the ancient Greeks and Romans on their hillsides or in their domestic plots, with medieval monks in their physick gardens and with ladies in their potagers (ornamental kitchen gardens).

Herbs, therefore, are not to be treasured just for their practical properties alone, for they are highly decorative, too, and bring perfume and a sense of history and age-old tradition to any spot they are grown.

THE REAL THING
When considering growing herbs, it is best to buy from a specialist nursery to ensure that the plants you get are the real thing, and not related species that share the same common names. There are two varieties of catmint, for example: one a decorative garden plant and the other the true herb. Finding out the respective botanical names avoids any confusion and will guide you to the correct choice: the garden species is *Nepeta x faassenii*, while the herb is *Nepeta cataria*.

Tarragon is another herb that can be misleading. There are two varieties: French and Russian. French tarragon has a delicate, sweet flavour that is particularly delicious with chicken. Russian tarragon, on the other hand, has a stronger and less pleasant flavour and much coarser leaves, yet is sometimes sold as French.

LOOKALIKES
When picking herbs, always choose those plants whose identity you are absolutely sure of – this is one reason why it is best to grow your own herbs, rather than pick any growing wild – and avoid experimentation with unfamiliar plants. Some plants traditionally used medicinally and as beauty aids are now known to be poisonous, and some poisonous plants have an uncanny – but dangerous – resemblance to others that are harmless.

For example, deadly nightshade, Atropa belladonna or 'beautiful lady,' is said to have acquired its botanical name because Italian

ladies once touched their eyes with it in order to enlarge their pupils and so make their eyes more alluring. Another tradition, however, says that it was used by an Italian poisoner to kill beautiful ladies, for in large doses, deadly nightshade is highly toxic.

Another innocent-looking plant, which resembles cow parsley and, to a degree, sweet cicely, is hemlock. Hemlock juice is a potent poison and is said to have killed the Greek philosopher Socrates.

An attractive collection of herbs is a boon to any garden.

S A F E T Y   R U L E S

When it comes to using herbs, there are several general rules to bear in mind.

Never use an unfamiliar herb or one whose properties you don't know. Remember that culinary herbs are safest.

If your symptoms persist for more than a couple of days, do not continue relying just on herbal remedies to relieve them. Consult your doctor to get an accurate diagnosis so that appropriate treatment can be given.

When taking herbal remedies, always start small – take smaller-than-normal doses initially to check for anyadverse reaction.

Always consult your doctor before taking any herbal remedy during pregnancy, or if you are suffering from any long-term condition.

Do not continue taking herbal remedies indefinitely without seeking professional advice either from your doctor or a qualified herbalist.

Herb Directory

HERB DIRECTORY

Before discussing the main points to consider when planning to grow and use herbs, we will first take a look at some of the best-known and most popular herbs – those you will most likely wish to include in your herb beds. The herb directory following provides information on 31 herbs, listed alphabetically by their botanical name for ease of reference. Each entry contains the plant's common name, together with details on its history and characteristics, how to grow and care for your herbs and the ways in which you can use them.

UNDERSTANDING THE SYMBOLS

TYPES

Hardy Perennial

Half-hardy Perennial

Hardy Annual

Half-hardy Annual

Shrub/sub-shrub

Hardy Biennial

POSITION

Prefers full sun

Prefers partial/filtered sun

Prefers shade

Requires wide spacing

SOIL TYPE

Well-drained

Moist

Sandy/dry

PROPAGATION

Division

Cuttings

Seeds

PARTS USED

Leaf

Flowers/seed

Root

USES

Culinary

Medicinal

Cosmetic

Decorative

Aromatic

PESTS/DISEASES

Fungus

Slugs/Snails

Mildew

Root rot

Aphids

HOW TO USE THE HERB DIRECTORY

Each herb entry is divided into four sections, explained below. The symbols provide essential information at a glance.

Symbols for 'Position' and 'Soil Type' show recommended placement. Plants can thrive in different soils and with different quantities of sunlight depending on factors such as climate. Only experience will tell.

HISTORY

This section describes the origin and historical uses of each plant, giving details of any special significance placed on the herb during the centuries.

CHARACTERISTICS

Gives details on the type and appearance of the herb, describing leaves, flowers and how it grows. Particular characteristics, such as flavour and fragrance are also provided.

GROWING TIPS

Describes suitable soil types, sunlight requirements and spacing needs of each plant, together with details of susceptibility to pests or diseases. Any special requirements or tips are included.

HOW TO USE

Gives tips on harvesting, together with summary of common uses, whether culinary, medicinal, or both.

TYPES

POSITION

SOIL TYPE

PROPAGATION

PARTS USED

USES

Yarrow

YARROW

Achillea millefolium

Used for centuries to treat wounds, and still in use as a medicinal plant today, its pretty clusters of flowers make yarrow an attractive ornamental plant as well.

HISTORY

Since ancient times, yarrow has been used to treat wounds. In fact its botanical name derives from the Greek hero, Achilles, who was said to have used yarrow to heal the battle wounds of his soldiers. Yarrow also features in rituals of divination in many parts of the world, most famously in the Chinese *I Ching*, where the stalk is used in the consultation.

CHARACTERISTICS

A hardy perennial, Yarrow can grow to a height of 90cm/36 inches, depending on particular species. Yarrow has a thick main stalk, branching into long ferny leaves. Flat clusters of small flowers, in a variety of colours, bloom between midsummer and autumn.

Bitter in both taste and aroma, yarrow can be taken internally to treat various ailments, although excessive use can produce allergic reactions.

Yarrow plants attract many beneficial insects, including ladybirds and tiny wasps which feed on harmful pests such as aphids.

GROWING TIPS

Yarrow should be planted in well-drained soil in full sunlight, although it will grow successfully in most soil types. Both sowing from seed or by division should take place in spring. Yarrow has a tendency to take over any available space in the garden, so should be grown in a container if space is limited. Allow at least 20cm/8 inches between plants.

HOW TO USE

Plants should be harvested when flowers are fully open. The whole stem should be cut and hung upside down to dry. As yarrow flowers retain their colour well after drying, they make a decorative addition to floral arrangements.

A poultice of yarrow leaves will help stem the flow of blood from minor scrapes and grazes, so is an ideal herb to have on hand for first aid. Yarrow tea can ease menstrual pain, ease feverish illnesses and relieve nervous complaints such as tension and upset stomachs.

Yarrow can also be used cosmetically to reduce oiliness in both skin and hair, and has been used as a wash for fair hair for thousands of years.

GARLIC

Allium sativum

Sharing with other members of the onion family the familiar compound bulb covered with a fine husk, the distinctive aroma and flavour of garlic make this an indispensable culinary herb.

HISTORY

Originating in Asia, garlic has been used medicinally, and as a culinary ingredient, for many thousands of years. Its use became widespread throughout other countries, and it features particularly in the cuisine of France and Italy. For centuries garlic was thought to have the power to ward off evil spirits – particularly vampires, a belief fostered by a multitude of books and films. Today its perceived beneficial properties are largely medicinal.

CHARACTERISTICS

A hardy perennial, garlic plants can grow to a height of 60cm/24 inches. Each plant has a stiff, straight stalk, from which grows long, bladed, bright green leaves. The stem is topped by a flower head formed by a cluster of tiny white or pink flowers. A garlic bulb contains a number of cloves, the size and quantity of which are determined by the specific variety grown, and also the climate.

The flavour and aroma of garlic are distinctive and familiar to almost everyone. As with size and quantity, the pungency of the flavour is largely determined by variety and growing conditions and temperature. Some garlic varieties are very strong, while others are sweeter and milder.

GROWING TIPS

Garlic bulbs should be planted in autumn or winter, in well-drained soil with plenty of sunshine. A moist soil is ideal, although plants can thrive in a drier soil if well-composted. Bulbs should be spaced around 20cm/8 inches apart, and should be planted at a depth of about 2.5cm/1 inch.

HOW TO USE

Garlic bulbs should be harvested in late summer to early autumn, and should be allowed to dry in the sun before being stored. The cloves can then be placed in a cool, dry place, or preserved in olive oil for a delicious dressing.

Cloves of garlic, crushed or chopped, make a delicious flavouring for many dishes, including meats, poultry, sauces and as a seasoning. If the aftertaste or lingering smell of garlic is a problem, chewing parsley leaves can reduce the effect.

Medicinally, garlic helps lower cholesterol levels and high blood pressure. It can also be taken internally to relieve colds and bronchial ailments and used externally to ease skin complaints such as acne.

TYPES

POSITION

SOIL TYPE

PROPAGATION

PARTS USED

USES

TYPES

POSITION

SOIL TYPE

PROPAGATION

PARTS USED

USES

PESTS/DISEASES

CHIVES

Allium schoenoprasum

Chives form part of the onion family, and as such are some of the most widely used herbs in the world. Their delicate flavour makes the suitable for use in most dishes, and as they are also one of the easiest herbs to grow, they will make an invaluable addition to your garden.

HISTORY

Native to Europe, and cultivated since the 16th century, chives are the only onion species that grow wild in North America. Used in cooking since ancient times, the delicate flavour of chives has made them primarily associated with salads and garnishes, rather than in cooked dishes.

CHARACTERISTICS

A hardy perennial, growing up to 45cm/18 inches tall, chives grow in clumps, generally of around five or six plants. Leaves are long, narrow and grass-like, and the distinctive pink or mauve globe-like flowers bloom in late spring or early summer. The flavour and scent of chives are more delicate than that of other onion types.

GROWING TIPS

Plant chives either as seeds in spring, or by division in either autumn or spring. Chives require full sun and a moist, well-drained soil. Chives are hardier than some other members of the allium family, and can tolerate wetter conditions. As chives can spread quite easily, it is a good idea to divide them every two to three years to prevent them becoming too squashed together. Groups of chives should be planted around 25cm/10 inches apart.

HOW TO USE

Leaves can be snipped for use fresh at any time during the growing period. Flowers should be picked soon after they have opened for use as garnishes.

Chives are not ideally suited for drying, as the already delicate flavour is soon lost. However, leaves or flowers can be frozen in ice cubes if you wish to store them for later use.

Chive leaves and flowers are most mostly used in salads or as garnishes. If you wish to use them in cooking, you will need to use larger quantities than for other onion types to gain a flavour.

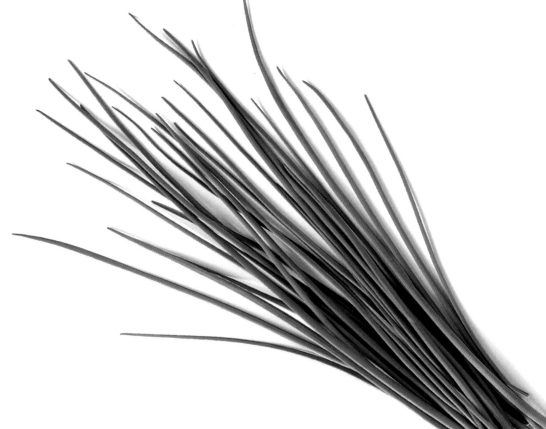

DILL

Anethum graveolens

One of the most versatile of herbs, dill is primarily used in cooking, although its mild medicinal properties make it ideal for those with sensitive stomachs. It has the added benefit of being very easy to grow.

HISTORY

The use of dill as a medicinal herb has been recorded since Biblical times, with a mention in the holy Jewish law, or Talmud. Its use was widespread throughout the Middle East and India, and was eventually introduced to Europe, like so many herbs, by the Romans.

CHARACTERISTICS

Dill is a perennial which can lay claim to a certain hardiness. It can grow to 100cm/40 inches high, with a spread of around 30cm/12 inches. Stems are green and hollow and branch out into fine, feathery leaves. Flowers appear around the middle of summer, and are formed into round, flat clusters of tiny yellow florets, which are very attractive to bees.

The leaf flavour is quite sharp and similar to that of parsley, while the seeds are almost bitter in taste.

GROWING TIPS

Dill can be easily grown from seed sown in late spring. Seeds should be sown in place, as dill does not take particularly well to transplanting. Seeds should be sown at intervals of 3 weeks, to ensure a constant fresh supply. Dill requires full sunlight, and can thrive as well in poorer, drier soils as in moist, drained soils. To allow comfortable spread, dill plants should be spaced around 25cm/10 inches apart.

HOW TO USE

Leaves can be cut at any time during the growing season for use fresh. For drying, leaves should be harvested just before flowers bloom. Seeds should be gathered in summer and dried for use in infusions or pickled. Whole seedheads should be wrapped in brown paper and stored, while whole stems for drying can be hung upside down. Leaves can also be frozen in ice cubes.

Dill can be used in pickling, or as an accompaniment to fish dishes. Dill is a tasty addition to most leaf vegetable dishes and salads.

Dill has a long history of use as an aid to digestive disorders, particularly colic in babies.

TYPES

POSITION

SOIL TYPE

PROPAGATION

PARTS USED

USES

Dill

TYPES

POSITION

SOIL TYPE

PROPAGATION

PARTS USED

USES

PESTS/DISEASES

TARRAGON

Artemisia dracunculus

Traditionally associated with French cuisine, tarragon forms one of the ingredients of the classic *fines herbes* mixture. Often difficult to grow outdoors, tarragon makes an ideal pot herb.

HISTORY

Native to southern Europe, the botanical name for tarragon derives from an old folkloric belief that it was a cure for poisonous stings and bites – hence its old common name of 'dragon herb'. As well as being used in cookery, tarragon was also used by herbalists in the past to relieve toothache. Today, however, it is largely regarded as a culinary herb only.

CHARACTERISTICS

A hardy perennial, growing up to 60cm/24 inches tall and with a spread of about half this, tarragon needs at least 60cm/24 inches between plants. Dark green, grass-like leaves grow longer at the base of the plant, becoming smaller towards the stem tip. Tiny white flowers grow at the tips towards the end of summer. Tasting and smelling a little like aniseed, tarragon has a distinctive bite to its flavour.

GROWING TIPS

Tarragon is best grown from cuttings or young seedlings. These should be transplanted in spring or early summer. Cuttings should be taken in autumn, and should be tended indoors during the winter months. Growing tarragon in pots is a good idea, as these can be brought indoors for

protection if your winters are particularly harsh. Tarragon needs moist, well-drained soil in full sunlight to thrive.

HOW TO USE

Leaves can be snipped at any time during the growing season for use fresh. Whole branches should be cut for drying, and micro waved for best results, as the flavour can diminish if drying is too slow. Freezing will retain more of the flavour.

The strong flavour of tarragon means that little needs to be added to dishes. Sprinkle leaves on salads, or add to stocks and casseroles particularly chicken dishes. To avoid the flavour becoming overpowering, it is best to add tarragon shortly before the end of the cooking period.

BORAGE

Borage officinalis

The cool flavour of borage, together with its attractive blue flowers, make it a popular plant for herb enthusiasts.

HISTORY

European in origin, borage was particularly used during the Middle Ages in central and southern regions both as a flavouring for wine, and as a vegetable substitute when ordinary crops were poor. Since ancient times it had been held to lift the spirits, praised by Pliny, and later recorded by John Gerard in *The Herball, or Generall Historie of Plantes (1597)*.

CHARACTERISTICS

This hardy annual grows up to 1 metre/40 inches high, with a spread of around 25cm/10 inches. The veiny, broad leaves are covered in fine hairs, which can grow straggly and untidy. These leaves have a cool, cucumber-like flavour. The blue, star-shaped flowers are particularly
attractive and grow in clusters; beginning to bloom in midsummer. Like bergamot, borage is extremely attractive to bees.

GROWING TIPS

Moist well-drained soil in full sun will produce thriving borage plants. Borage will grow in poorer soils, but plants may not reach their full growth potential. Borage self-sows easily, and needaround 60 square cm/24 square inches around each plant. Correct moisture level is important for a healthy plant. In very dry conditions, borage may develop mildew, while in soggy conditions, root rot may appear. Seeds should be sown directly into your bed in spring. Transplanting borage is not recommended.

HOW TO USE

Leaves can be used fresh or dried, and should be harvested in spring or early summer just as the plant is flowering. Fresh or frozen leaves bring a delightful fresh taste to summer wine-based drinks, and can also be added lightly to salads.

Flowers should be gathered as they open, and used to garnish salads, frozen for decorative ice cubes or crystallized for decorative desserts. Borage is little used medicinally today, although an infusion may be taken to ease fevers or throat irritations. A borage poultice can alleviate sprains and bruises.

Dried borage leaves should be kept for no longer than one year, as the flavour and properties deteriorate with time.

TYPES

POSITION

SOIL TYPE

PROPAGATION

PARTS USED

USES

PESTS/DISEASES

Borage

TYPES

POSITION

SOIL TYPE

PROPAGATION

PARTS USED

USES

MUSTARD

Brassica spp.

One of the most distinctive and easy to grow herbs, mustard must evoke childhood memories in most people of growing mustard seeds in small pots or on blotting paper.

HISTORY

Mustard's popularity as a condiment can be traced back to ancient Greece and Rome, where mustard seeds were crushed and mixed with wine. Its use in medicine was first recorded by the Chinese in the seventh century.

CHARACTERISTICS

Of the three main types of mustard; nigra (black mustard), alba (white mustard) and juncea (brown mustard), it is the latter which is most commonly used. Juncea grows to a top height of 1.5 metres/60 inches, so is more suitable for domestic cultivation than its relatives which can grow much taller. Mustard has fine stems, ending in tiny leaves and four-petalled yellow flowers.

GROWING TIPS

A hardy perennial, mustard can be grown in well-drained soil and in full sunshine. Seeds are best sown in spring. The alba variety is most commonly grown indoors, as in the mustard and cress' combinations grown by school children the world over. Whether planted indoors or out, mustard is an easy herb to cultivate.

HOW TO USE

Seed pods should be gathered in late summer, just before they finish ripening. The ripening process will continue after they have been picked. Once dried, pods can be stored indefinitely in a sealed container. The seeds themselves have little bite. The traditional hot mustard flavour comes from the mixing of the dry mustard powder with water. Cold water only should be used when mixing mustard powder, as hot water ruins the flavour.

As well as creating a wide variety of mustard relishes, mustard leaves can be added to salads, and seeds can also be added to curries and pickles.

Medicinally, a mustard poultice is a popular and effective remedy to relieve muscular pain, arthritis, rheumatism and chilblains. A mustard foot bath is held to ease colds and headaches.

Care should be taken, as mustard also has irritant properties. Sensitive skins may react to prolonged contact with mustard, while taking too much internally may lead to stomach irritation.

Marigold

Calendula officinalis

With their vibrant yellow-orange flowers, marigolds are a distinctive feature of many country gardens.

History

Recorded in use in Eastern and European cultures since ancient times, both as a colourant for material and as a medicinal herb, the marigold was once considered a holy flower by early pagans. Indeed, Christianity later absorbed this belief, dedicating the beautiful golden flowers to the Virgin Mary.

Dried petals became popular as spices during the Middle Ages.

Characteristics

A hardy annual, the marigold has a long flowering period, generally from summer through to the first frosty spell, and plants can grow up to 30cm/12 inches, although variants may reach twice this height. Plant spread is about half this height. Leaves are narrow and pointed, and slightly hairy. Flowers are a vivid orange or yellow, and petals have a slightly bitter flavour. Marigolds have little fragrance.

Growing Tips

Marigolds can be grown from seed outdoors, or transplanted as seedlings after growing inside. In each case, late spring is best for planting, when the soil has warmed. They require full sunlight, although in warmer climates they will grow if placed in partial shade. Soil should be well-drained, and moist, although poorer soils can be acceptable as long as plants have direct sunlight. Space marigolds around 20cm/8 inches apart. To prolong flowering, remove dead heads regularly.

How to Use

Marigold flowers should be harvested just after they have fully opened. Late morning, when dew has dried, is the best time for this. For best results, cut the stem at the joint nearest the flower head. Petals can be used fresh, or dried. To dry, place petals separately between sheets of brown paper, and keep in a shady area. When dry, place in a dark, dry place, in an airtight container. Marigold petals can also be dried in a microwave.

Petals can be added fresh to salads for an unusual effect, or dried to add colour to rice, stocks or dairy products. Whole flowers also make attractive garnishes.

Primarily regarded for its cosmetic applications, marigold can be used in moisturising skin creams or washes to condition or lighten hair. Petals can also be used to ease eye and skin irritations, and can help heal minor cuts and abrasions.
A marigold infusion can also soothe stomach complaints. Marigold treatments should not be used during pregnancy.

TYPES

POSITION

SOIL TYPE

PROPAGATION

PARTS USED

USES

PESTS/DISEASES

TYPES

POSITION

SOIL TYPE

PROPAGATION

PARTS USED

USES

PESTS/DISEASES

FEVERFEW

Chrysanthemum parthenium

A tansy variation, sharing the familiar white and gold flowers of the daisy family, feverfew is a decorative plant all year round.

HISTORY

Native to southern Europe, but introduced to temperate areas such as North America and England, the medicinal qualities of feverfew have been recognised for centuries. Along with other tansy plants, feverfew had its place in early Christian rituals, featuring as a cleansing herb partaken after the traditional Lenten feast.

CHARACTERISTICS

A hardy perennial, reaching 60cm/24 inches in height, feverfew produces numerous daisy-like flowers throughout summer until mid autumn. Even after the flowers have died away, towards the end of the year, the feverfew plant remains attractive due to its dense and bushy leaves. Varying in colour from pale through golden-green, the leaves are segmented and can grow up to 8cm/3 inches long. These leaves have an unpleasant, bitter flavour, making them unsuitable for use in cooking.

GROWING TIPS

Thriving in even the poorest soils, as long as it is well-drained, feverfew should be planted in direct sunlight where soil is poor, otherwise partial shade is suitable. Seeds should be planted in spring or autumn, while cuttings can be transplanted in spring or summer. Dead heads should be regularly removed, as feverfew sows itself easily. Plants should be spaced 30cm/12 inches apart. Feverfew is susceptible to aphids, so plants should be inspected regularly.

HOW TO USE

Leaves should be harvested before the flowers bloom if they are to be dried for medicinal use. For use fresh, pick leaves or stems just as plants are flowering. Stems can be dried by hanging upside down. Leaves can be frozen in ice cubes.

Feverfew is particularly effective for relieving migraine headaches. Leaves can be taken either in an infusion, or whole, fresh or dried. Some additive, such as honey; is recommended to mask the bitter taste. A daily dose of around three leaves a day in suggested to lessen the effect, and frequency of such headaches. Feverfew can also relieve the pain of arthritis and menstrual cramps.

CORIANDER

Coriandrum sativum

A popular culinary herb, featuring particularly in Asian and Central American dishes, coriander is an easy to grow plant, and ideally suited for those just beginning to cultivate a herb garden.

HISTORY

Well-known among the ancient cultures of Europe, Asia and South America, coriander has been used for centuries in both medicine and cooking, although today its medicinal qualities are little exploited. It was first introduced to England by the Romans, and enjoyed considerable popularity through Tudor times. Such was its widespread usage, it was among the precious plants taken by the early settlers to the 'New World' of North America.

CHARACTERISTICS

A hardy annual, growing to 60cm/24 inches, and with a spread of 22cm/9 inches, coriander leaves are flat and fern-like, similar in appearance to some types of parsley. Pink or white flowers grow in clusters, and appear towards the end of summer. An aromatic plant, the leaves have a sharp taste, while the seeds are sweeter, and spicier.

GROWING TIPS

Coriander can be planted from spring through summer. It will need full sunlight if planted earlier in the year, while filtered sunlight or some shade is needed as the weather gets warmer. Coriander does not take well to transplanting. It is best to plant from seed, directly into your chosen bed. Soil should be well-drained and moist. Coriander plants self-sow with ease. While this ensures a continual supply, stems can be pinched as buds appear, to reduce plant spread. Allow around 20cm/8 inches around each plant. Ensure soil is well-drained, as coriander plants can be susceptible to root-rot or wilting if too much moisture accumulates.

HOW TO USE

Leaves should be gathered when young – usually when the plant is around 15cm/6 inches tall. For storage they are best frozen, rather than dried. Seeds should be fully ripe before harvesting.

Leaves are commonly used in curries, Mexican dishes such as salsas, chutneys, or fresh in salads. Seeds also feature in curries and casseroles, and have a particularly piquant flavour when roasted. The root can be cooked as a vegetable, although the flavour may not be to everyone's taste.

Although not used so much in herbal medicine today, coriander seeds can be chewed to aid digestive complaints, and a poultice of bruised seeds can relieve joint pain and also haemorrhoids.

TYPES

POSITION

SOIL TYPE

PROPAGATION

PARTS USED

USES

Coriander

TYPES

POSITION

SOIL TYPE

PROPAGATION

PARTS USED

USES

FENNEL

Foeniculum vulgare

The lacy leaves and yellow florets of fennel make this a particularly attractive herb, ideal for growing as a background plant in a border. To complement its visual appeal, it is delicious in many recipes, as well as having medicinal benefits.

HISTORY

Native to Mediterranean regions, and particularly a feature of Italian cuisine, fennel has been naturalised to temperate areas around the world, including parts of California. Its use in England dates back before the Norman conquest.
In medieval times it was a popular flavouring, especially with fish, but the subtle flavour was such that fennel seeds were often chewed during Lent, to ward off hunger pangs while fasting.

CHARACTERISTICS

A hardy perennial, fennel can grow to a height of 1.5 m/5 ft, with a spread easily reaching half its height. The soft, feathery leaves of fennel can easily overpower your border, which is why they are best planted behind other plants, and with plenty of space to thrive. Stems are ridged, forming many branches, and are pale green in colour. The florets of tiny yellow flowers can grow to 15cm/6 inches wide, and appear in midsummer. The seeds form in late summer, and are flat, oval and ridged. Fennel leaves have a more subtle, delicate flavour than the seeds, but both have an aroma and taste a little like that of aniseed.

GROWING TIPS

Although seeds can be sown in autumn, spring is the best time of year for planting fennel seeds. These can be planted directly into your chosen site. As a native of the warm, Mediterranean region, fennel plants need plenty of sunshine, although if they are to be placed within the full glare of the sun, some shade is acceptable. Fennel needs a moist soil, but one that drains well, as overwatering can be harmful. As fennel plants spread widely, take care with spacing. Allow at least 15cm/6 inches between plants. If your winters are particularly harsh, you may find you need to winter your bulbs in a bucket of dry soil. Remove them around the beginning of November, and store somewhere cool and dry.

HOW TO USE

Leaves can be picked at any time during the growing season, while the leaf base is most tender during spring. Roots should be harvested in autumn and dried. Seeds can be used unripe, in fresh dishes, or ripe, for drying. Ripe seeds should be collected before they fall, and dried in a paper bag.

Fennel leaves are particularly popular in fish dishes, although they are a delicious accompaniment to pork, pasta dishes and salads. Stems can be cooked as a vegetable, although as they lose their flavour quickly when heated, should be added to recipes shortly before serving. Fennel seeds are used as a spice, particularly in Eastern recipes.

Fennel also has several medicinal qualities. An infusion of crushed seeds aids digestive problems both in adults or children, and can also be gargled for mouth and throat complaints. The seeds can also be chewed to sweeten breath.

Although fennel has adapted to climates somewhat cooler than their native Mediterranean region, some extra care must be taken if your winters are harsh.

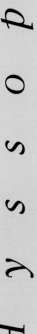

TYPES

POSITION

SOIL TYPE

PROPAGATION

PARTS USED

USES

HYSSOP

Hyssopus officinalis

An attractive, flowering herb, sharing many of the characteristics of the mint family to which it belongs, hyssop is an excellent herb for beginners to plant, as it is relatively easy to grow, and reasonably hardy.

HISTORY

Mentioned in pre-Christian texts, and once believed to have purification properties, hyssop is native to parts of Europe and Asia, although now grown throughout the world. Once one of the most well-known herbs for its medicinal uses, its popularity has declined somewhat in later centuries.

CHARACTERISTICS

A hardy perennial, hyssop reaches a height of up to 90cm/36 inches tall and can spread to around 40cm/16 inches. Slim, pointed leaves issue from a tall branching stem, and flowers bloom during midsummer to autumn. These form into tall spikes of delicate blue flowers. The aroma of the plant is somewhat minty, with a hint of bitterness.

GROWING TIPS

Hyssop prefers a dry, well-drained soil, with plenty of sunlight. Seeds should be sown in autumn or spring, while cuttings can be planted in summer. For best growth, plants should be cut well back in spring. Plants should be spaced around 30cm/12 inches apart.

HOW TO USE

Leaves should be picked before the flowers bloom. Snip individual leaves for immediate use, or cut whole stems for drying. This is best done by hanging upside down. Flowers should be picked just as the buds have opened.

Hyssop has quite a strong flavour, so should be added sparingly to dishes. Leaves can be added to salads, and both leaves and flowers can be included in stuffing, soups and casseroles.

Hyssop's main medicinal use is in relieving bronchial congestions and inflammations, or as a gargle for sore throats.

Hyssop's distinctive aroma make it particularly suitable for inclusion in pot pourris and dried floral arrangements.

BAY

Laurus nobilis

Bay is a most versatile herb, adding a delicious flavour to dishes, and decorative in both garnishes and indoor arrangements.

HISTORY

Asian in origin, Bay was one of the most widely used herbs in classical civilisations. Indeed, the traditional laureate, or circlet of leaves, still known today as a symbol of victory and valour, has its origins in ancient Greece and Rome, where a crown of bay laurel leaves was presented to those who excelled in martial or intellectual arts. Although bay has been used historically for medicinal purposes, today it features most usually in the kitchen.

CHARACTERISTICS

An evergreen shrub, a bay tree can reach over 7 m/20 feet tall, and 2 m/6 feet wide.
The distinctive leaves are dark green, long and glossy, making this an ornamental, as well as useful plant. Stems are woody and grey, and make an ideal base for herbal and floral arrangements. Flowers bloom in late spring and are small and yellow. Sweetly aromatic, the leaves have a strong, distinctive taste, and retain their flavour well during cooking.

GROWING TIPS

Bay should be planted in spring, from cuttings taken in early summer. It requires a moist, well-drained soil, and prefers partial shade. They can suffer in harsh winter conditions, so need to be in a sheltered position in the garden. If your winters are particularly severe, it is a good idea to plant bay in a pot, which can be brought indoors during the colder months. A potted bay is particularly decorative, and easy to manage as it will grow to no more than 2 to 3 m/6 to 8 feet in height.

HOW TO USE

Leaves should be collected in summer and dried whole, although their flavour will diminish if kept for longer than one year. To dry, hang in a warm, dry place, in bundles.

Bay leaves are the most important ingredient of a classic bouquet garni, and are most usually added to soups, sauces and stocks. They can also add a delicious taste to desserts. The flavour is potent, and a single leaf or half leaf is usually sufficient for an average sized dish.

A bay leaf infusion can relieve indigestion, colic and flatulence. Leaves can also be used on sprains and bruises.

Bay is also a staple ingredient of herbal pot pourris, where the crushed leaves add a distinctive aroma. Bay leaves can also deter weevils if placed in containers of flour or other dried goods.

TYPES

POSITION

SOIL TYPE

PROPAGATION

PARTS USED

USES

Bay

TYPES

POSITION

SOIL TYPE

PROPAGATION

PARTS USED

USES

PESTS/DISEASES

LAVENDER

Lavandula augustifolia

Lavender must surely be one of the world's most popular plants. Attractive to look at, with a beautiful scent and a wide range of uses from the cosmetic to the medicinal, it is certainly a must for any budding herbalist.

HISTORY

A native of Europe, lavender is now found in almost every part of the world. Used since ancient times as a basis for aromatic oils and perfumes, the sweet smell of dried lavender has been used to mask unpleasant aromas since the Middle Ages, where its scent was also believed to ward off pestilence and disease. A popular ingredient of Victorian pomanders, and still the mainstay of many an air freshener or pot pourri today.

CHARACTERISTICS

Lavender is a hardy perennial shrub which grows to a height of up to 90cm/36 inches, although some dwarf varieties, popularly used as edgings or borders, reach a maximum height of 20cm/6 inches. A thick stem grows from a cluster of spiky, narrow leaves, which can grow straggly and untidy if left untrimmed. Tiny purple or sometimes white flowers form in spikes at the top of the stems, and appear around midsummer. The scent of these flowers is particularly appealing, and attracts bees in the garden.

GROWING TIPS

Lavender prefers dry, well-drained soils, and thrives in full sunshine. Plants should be grown from seed in spring, from cuttings in late spring or early autumn, or from divisions in spring or summer. Allow 30cm/12 inches between each plant. To avoid leaves becoming straggly, pruning is recommended in spring.

HOW TO USE

Flowers should be picked as they open, and either dried or used fresh. Dried lavender retains its aroma for many months, and for best results whole stems should be left to dry in a cool, dark place. Dried petals can then be sprinkled into pot pourri, tied or sewn into sachets for use as room or drawer fresheners.

A lavender tea can be brewed to calm nerves, and a pillow filled with lavender can help induce sleep. The scent of lavender is also cooling and refreshing, and lavender water is often used when travelling.

The scent of lavender is said to be a good insect repellent. An oil distillation can be applied to the skin for this purpose. A lavender infusion can also relieve the itching of insect bites.

LOVAGE

Levisticum officinale

Similar in both taste and appearance to celery, lovage traditionally holds a place in herbal medicine, but is today more likely to be used in the kitchen.

HISTORY

Used by the ancient Greeks and Romans, and native to southern Europe, lovage enjoyed a widespread popularity until the Middle Ages, when its usage began to dwindle. Used predominantly as a stock vegetable, and for its medicinal properties of soothing upset stomachs, lovage was also once used in love potions, hence its other common name of 'love parsley'.

CHARACTERISTICS

A hardy perennial growing to a height of 2 m/80 inches and half this in width, lovage has a straight, ribbed stalk which branches only at the top. Here cluster the small, jagged leaves and the tiny groups of yellowish flowers that appear in summer.

GROWING TIPS

Lovage should be grown from seed sown in autumn, or by division in spring. Moist, well-drained soil and partial sunlight are ideal conditions. As these plants spread quite widely, allow 60 square cm/24 square inches around each plant.

HOW TO USE

Leaves can be picked at any time during the growing season for use fresh. For drying, leaves should be picked shortly before the plant flowers. Seed heads should be picked in late summer and wrapped in brown paper as they ripen. Lovage loses its flavour quickly, so for best results dry in the microwave.

Leaves can be used as a substitute for celery – in salads, soups and stews. Chopped stems can be treated like a vegetable, although they can be very tough and fibrous.

Lovage has antiseptic properties, so can be used to treat and clean minor wounds. An infusion can be taken to relieve indigestion, colic and cystitis.

TYPES

POSITION

SOIL TYPE

PROPAGATION

PARTS USED

USES

TYPES

POSITION

SOIL TYPE

PROPAGATION

PARTS USED

USES

PESTS/DISEASES

LEMON BALM

Melissa officinalis

The fresh, citrus scent of lemon balm make it a particularly delightful garden plant. Bees are attracted to the sharp aroma, and the lemon tang of both the scent and flavour make for a delicious tisane or herbal tea.

HISTORY

Although now widely grown throughout the world, lemon balm originated in southern Europe. It enjoyed great popularity in the Middle Ages, and was one of the highly prized herbs taken to North America by the early settlers. Lemon balm has been brewed as a herbal tea for many centuries, and was widely believed to have a soothing, almost sedative effect. For this reason it was very popular among ladies of a nervous disposition during Victorian times. Even today it is held to be a relaxing drink.

CHARACTERISTICS

Lemon balm is a hardy perennial, growing to a height of 60cm/24 inches, with a similar spread. A member of the mint family, it has the characteristic square stem and coarse, toothed leaves which range in colour from yellow-green to dark green. Tiny white flowers bloom in summer.

GROWING TIPS

Lemon balm should be grown in moist, well-drained soil in the hottest part of your garden. Spring or autumn are the best planting times; either by sowing seeds, cuttings or by division.

Lemon balm can spread easily and rapidly, so if you wish to keep its growth in check, it may be an idea to grow it in pots or containers.

HOW TO USE

Plants should be harvested as flowering begins. Leaves can be used fresh, or stems snipped for drying for use in infusions or tinctures. Dry leaves and stems by placing on a rack, or freeze leaves in ice cubes for use in mint teas.

Lemon balm makes a refreshing and relaxing tea or tisane, and can relieve ailments predominantly caused by stress, such as nervous headaches or upset stomachs.

In cooking lemon balm is primarily used as a fresh salad ingredient, although leaves can be added to soups and stocks for a fresh minty taste.

Lemon balm is also used in aromatherapy, and as a prime ingredient of many pot pourris.

Lemon Balm

TYPES

POSITION

SOIL TYPE

PROPAGATION

PARTS USED

USES

PESTS/DISEASES

M i n t

MINT

Mentha spp.

The mint family is a large one, comprising many different varieties. Some share more similarities than others, and these we have grouped together. Each is popular and widely used throughout the world.

HISTORY

Used widely by the ancient Greeks and Romans, most mint varieties are native to the Mediterranean region, although some originated in parts of Asia. Mints now grow both wild and by cultivation in most countries, Two of the most popular varieties, peppermint and spearmint; were both introduced by the Romans, who are also credited with the creation of the ever-popular mint sauce.

CHARACTERISTICS

Mints are hardy perennials, and most types can reach a height of 45cm/18 inches with a 30cm/12 inch spread, although there will be some variation depending on specific variety. Mint stems tend to be somewhat square, and leaves range from oval to heart shaped, and range from pale to dark green in colour. Most end in a sharp point. Flowers bloom towards the end of summer, and form in spikes of tiny white, pink or purple flowers.

Each variety of mint differs in taste and scent. Apple mint, for example, as the name would suggest, is rather sweet in flavour, while peppermint is cooler and stronger.

GROWING TIPS

Mint is best grown from cuttings or bought from a nursery or garden centre, as It does not grow well from seed. A moist soil will help mints thrive, and although full sunshine will not be harmful, partial sunshine is recommended. As mints spread very quickly, both above ground and via roots, allow up to 60cm/24 inches between plants. Mint can easily take over a herb bed, so unless this is what you want, grow mint in separate beds, or in pots or containers.

HOW TO USE

Leaves can be snipped for use fresh or for drying throughout the growing season. Whole plants for drying should be cut just as flowering begins, and either hung upside down or laid on racks to dry.

Mint leaves are also ideally frozen in ice cubes.

Mints add a delicious flavour to many dishes. Fresh leaves can be added to salads, or to lamb, fish or vegetable dishes. A traditional mint sauce is a delicious accompaniment to lamb. Mint can also be added to summer drinks, jellies and desserts such as ice cream.

Medicinally, mint helps to soothe upset stomaches, indigestion and flatulence. An infusion of spearmint or peppermint can also help promote sleep.

Mint

B e r g a m o t

BERGAMOT

Monarda didyma

One of the most widely planted herbs for its distinctive appearance, bergamot is a beautiful feature of any ornamental herb garden.

HISTORY

Native to North America, and widely used as a medicinal stimulant by the Native Americans, particularly the Oswego tribe, near Lake Ontario; Bergamot holds a distinctive place in American history. Shortly before the American War of Independence, many households drank 'Oswego tea', as a protest against the British government's tax on imported teas.

CHARACTERISTICS

A hardy perennial, growing up to 1.5 m/3 feet in height, and spreading to over 30cm/12 inches wide. The leaves are dark-green, sometimes with a slight tinge of red. They are hairy with a tooth-edge. Flowers can be pink or purple, although it is the red variety that is most commonly grown. Flowers appear in midsummer, growing at the tip of the stem, and with distinctive tubular petals. Red bergamot has a citrus-like aroma, and is also known by the common name of 'bee-balm' as bees are particularly attracted to it.

GROWING TIPS

Bergamot prefers well-drained, sandy soil, in partial sun, although it will grow in full sun if kept moist. Seeds should be planted in spring; cuttings or divisions in late spring or summer. Bergamot spreads very quickly, and requires wide spacing. At least 60 square cm/24 square inches is required. If summers are particularly dry, bergamot is prone to powdery mildew.

HOW TO USE

Leaves should be cut for using fresh or drying before the flowers bloom in early summer. If drying the leaves, they can be either placed on racks to dry naturally, or micro waved. If you wish to dry the flowers, cut them just before they reach full bloom. These should then be hung to dry.

Bergamot flowers make attractive additions to salads, while the leaves continue to be brewed for teas. Bergamot tea is slightly similar in taste to Earl Grey. Although not used particularly as a medicinal herb, bergamot tea can be relaxing, and may well ease minor digestive ailments.

The dried flowers enhance decorative arrangements and pot pourris.

CATMINT

Nepeta cataria

Known more for the effect it has on cats than for its culinary uses, catmint also has a place in your herbal medicine chest.

HISTORY

Native to parts of Asia and Europe, catmint was once widely used in herbal remedies, particularly for the treatment of colds and chest complaints, as recorded by Gerard in his *Herball*. It has been used in Chinese herbal medicine for centuries.

CHARACTERISTICS

Catmint can grow to 90cm/36 inches tall, and can spread to around 40cm/16 inches. Catmint leaves are heart-shaped, with toothed edges, and both leaves and stems are lightly haired. Flowers bloom in spikes in midsummer, and colours range from white to purple. The most distinctive characteristic of catmint is its irresistible attraction for cats, which is why catmint, or catnip as it is often known, is a strong feature in many pet toys.

GROWING TIPS

Catmint requires a moist, well-drained soil, preferably in full sun. Seeds can be sown in spring or autumn, while division should take place in spring. You will need to cut back the plant at the end of the growing season to ensure a good crop the following year. Allow around 25cm/10 inches around each plant. Although susceptible to powdery mildew in very hot conditions, the main danger to catmint plants comes from the over-enthusiastic attention from cats! To prevent catmint being pawed, nibbled or rolled on, it is a good idea to protect your plants behind wire mesh.

HOW TO USE

Catmint is rarely used as a culinary herb, although a catnip tea can have a mild sedative effect to relieve stress or insomnia.

TYPES

POSITION

SOIL TYPE

PROPAGATION

PARTS USED

USES

PESTS/DISEASES

TYPES

POSITION

SOIL TYPE

PROPAGATION

PARTS USED

USES

PESTS/DISEASES

BASIL

Ocimum basilicum

Basil may well be the world's most popular herb. Almost every type of basil can be used in cooking, although sweet basil, the variety we look at here, is the most widely used, featuring in the cuisine of almost every culture. Easy to grow, sweet-smelling and delicious to taste, it could well be described as the perfect herb.

HISTORY

Basil originated in India, where it is still considered sacred by the Hindus, second only to the lotus. Most Hindu homes and temples have basil growing nearby, as it is believed to have a protective influence. From India, basil reached Europe by way of the Middle East. The Ancient cultures of Greece, Egypt and Rome prized basil greatly. Indeed the Greek name for basil, basilikon, means 'royal'.

CHARACTERISTICS

A half-hardy annual, basil can reach 60cm/24 inches tall. Leaf appearance varies according to type. Sweet basil has deep green, glossy leaves with smooth edges. Stems are somewhat woody, and often straggly. Basil flowers in spikes, generally white, and bloom between midsummer and autumn. Basil is particularly aromatic, with a fresh smell, with hints of mint and pepper. The taste is a delicious combination of sweet and spicy, making basil an ideal accompaniment to many dishes.

GROWING TIPS

Basil seeds should be sown in spring, and transplanted into pots or directly into a garden bed in the warmth of late spring or early summer. Shoot tips should be pinched to ensure bushy growth, and to prevent flowering. Basil prefers a moist, well drained soil, and needs plenty of sunlight. Basil is ideally suited to growing in pots, on a sunny windowsill, so is a good herb to choose if your space is limited. Basil requires a generous amount of spacing between plants – around 30 to 45 cm/12 to 18 inches is sufficient. Keep an eye out for aphids or slugs, and also the appearance of powdery mildew.

HOW TO USE

Basil should be harvested whole as plants are about to bloom – usually when they are around 25cm/10 inches tall. When cutting a stem, leave at least two leaves growing, so that new branches will form. Leaves can be picked throughout the growing season, and used fresh, or dried for later use. Seeds should be collected when ripe and dried for use in decoctions. Basil can be hung to dry, or frozen.

Basil is the key ingredient of the classic pesto sauce, and makes a fine accompaniment to tomatoes in salads. Its delicious flavour also works well with soups, vegetable dishes, chicken and duck.

Medicinally, a basil infusion can be taken internally to ease feverish illnesses such as colds and flu, as well as minor digestive problems. Basil is a stimulating herb, and can also be taken to relieve exhaustion, or added to a bath as a 'pick-me-up'.

Herb collection with basil

Marjoram

Origanum majorana

A mainstay of the herbal garden, with a variety of uses from culinary to medicinal, marjoram is often confused with oregano. However, the commercial oregano widely available is often a combination of several varieties of marjoram, rather than any one plant.

History

Native to Europe, and widely used since ancient times, marjoram was originally prized as a medicinal, rather than a culinary herb, and was believed by the ancient Greeks to aid the pains of childbirth. Nowadays it is more widely associated with cooking, although it still has a place in the herbal medicine chest.

Characteristics

A half-hardy perennial, marjoram can grow to around 45cm/18 inches tall, and spread to about half this. Marjoram has a long, green, somewhat woody stalk, which branches into delicate, oval leaves. Flowers bloom around the end of summer, and are clusters of tiny white or pink spikes. Marjoram has a delicate scent, and a sweetly spicy flavour.

Growing Tips

Marjoram thrives in dry, well-drained soil, and requires plenty of sunlight. Seeds should be sown in autumn or spring, cuttings planted in early summer, and divisions made in autumn or spring. Marjoram is susceptible to cold, wet conditions, and should be sheltered from the worst of the weather. To survive a harsh winter, marjoram will need care and attention. In fact, you may prefer to pot marjoram and bring indoors during the winter months.

How to Use

Plants should be cut as the flowering begins. Leaves can be snipped individually for use fresh, while whole stems should be gathered for drying. For best results, hang upside down to dry, or alternatively freeze leaves in butter or as ice cubes.

Fresh leaves should be added shortly before the end of cooking for the best flavour. They are delicious added to soups and pasta dishes or as a seasoning to most meat recipes.

An infusion can relieve bronchial congestion, menstrual cramps or indigestion, and can be applied externally to reduce pain of sprains or stiff joints.

TYPES

POSITION

SOIL TYPE

PROPAGATION

PARTS USED

USES

Marjoram

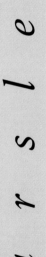

TYPES

POSITION

SOIL TYPE

PROPAGATION

PARTS USED

USES

PESTS/DISEASES

PARSLEY

Petroselinum crispum

This flat-leaved, curly variety of parsley is the most common, and the one found in grocery shops and vegetable gardens throughout the world. If someone is likely to have just one herb growing in their garden, the chances are that it will be parsley.

HISTORY

Originating in the Mediterranean regions, parsley has been recorded in use since the time of the ancient Greeks and Romans. Primarily a culinary herb, it was also used in certain ceremonies, and in some cases credited with healing properties.

CHARACTERISTICS

A hardy biennial, parsley is relatively low-growing, reaching a maximum height of about 30cm/12 inches, with a spread of about half this. Parsley is a particularly attractive plant, with distinctive curly leaves attached to a long stem. Flowers do not tend to appear until the spring of the second year, and when they do they are flat clusters of tiny yellowish flowers. Parsley has a distinctive fresh, slightly sweet flavour, and a scent to match.

GROWING TIPS

Parsley seeds can be sown directly into your beds between spring and autumn, and may take up to six weeks to germinate. A moist, well-drained soil in partial sunlight is ideal. As plants take such a long time to appear, you may wish to plant seeds in advance indoors, and then transplant. Parsley plants require around 25cm/10 inches of space around them.

Parsley is one of the easiest plants to grow if space is limited, as it thrives just as well in pots indoors as it does out in the open.

HOW TO USE

Plants should be allowed to grow at least 8 or 10 leaves before you begin to harvest them. After this, leaves can be plucked at any time for use fresh, or for drying. Leaves should be dried in the microwave for best flavour retention, or can be frozen on a baking tray. Almost every restaurant will use parsley as a garnish to dishes, but it

would be a shame to limit its uses in this way. An addition of fresh or dried parsley can add a subtle flavour to most savoury dishes, particularly sauces and fish recipes.

Parsley has little modern medical use, but can ease urinary and gastric discomfort. It should not be taken by pregnant women, or those suffering from kidney complaints.

ROSEMARY

Rosemarinus officinalis

A popular, easy to grow and long-lasting plant, rosemary has a history rich in folklore.

HISTORY

Native to the Mediterranean regions, rosemary has several folkloric associations. Sprigs of rosemary were given as keepsakes at both weddings and funerals for centuries, and even today rosemary is a symbol of remembrance, recalling Ophelia's speech from Shakespeare's *Hamlet*. Greek scholars were also once garlanded with rosemary during examinations, as it was also believed to aid memory.

CHARACTERISTICS

A half hardy perennial shrub, which can vary in height between 60 to120cm/24 to 48 inches and can spread almost as wide. The long, almost needle-like leaves grow from a stiff woody stem. These leaves are green on top with silver underneath. The delicate flowers, which are pink or purple, appear in twos or threes during spring or summer.

HOW TO USE

Harvest leaves and the flower tops in spring and summer, and either use fresh or dry. Full stems should be hung upside down to dry.

Rosemary is a traditional accompaniment to lamb dishes, either roasted, or in stews or casseroles. It can also be sprinkled over meat for grilling.

Dried rosemary makes an attractive indoor decoration, and can also be added to bathwater or hair rinses for a stimulating effect.

Rosemary is little used as a medicinal herb, although an infusion can alleviate the symptoms of nervous ailments such as stress, headaches and digestive problems.

TYPES

POSITION

SOIL TYPE

PROPAGATION

PARTS USED

USES

GROWING TIPS

Rosemary grows best from cuttings or bought seedlings, as seeds take a long time to germinate. Cuttings should be planted in early summer, in moist, well-drained soil and with full sunlight. If winters are particularly prone to harsh frosts, plant rosemary where it will be afforded some protection. If planting in beds, rosemary plants should be placed at least 60cm/24 inches apart. If planting in pots, make sure these are deep, and repot frequently.

Rosemary

SAGE

Salvia officinalis

TYPES

POSITION

SOIL TYPE

PROPAGATION

PARTS USED

USES

PESTS/DISEASES

There are hundreds of varieties of sage grown throughout the world, of which this variety is the most popular for use in cooking. Its fresh scent also makes it a pleasant addition to your garden.

HISTORY

Primarily known as a medicinal plant since classical times, hence its botanical name *Salvia*, meaning 'saviour', sage became popular as a culinary herb in the Middle Ages. Centuries ago, sage was believed to promote longevity, while the Ancient Egyptians believed it increased fertility. Introduced to North America by the early colonists, sage is now one of the most common, and traditional, cooking herbs in most countries.

CHARACTERISTICS

A hardy perennial shrub, Sage can grow to a height of 1 m/40 inches tall with a 30cm/12 inch spread. The somewhat woody stems branch into long oval, grey-ish leaves. Flowers appear around midsummer. These range from white through blue and pink, and grow in vertical clusters of small, tubular blooms. Sage has a particularly appealing scent and flavour, slightly warm and with a hint of camphor.

GROWING TIPS

Plant sage in a well-drained soil, with plenty of sunlight. Seeds can take time to germinate, so for best results transplant cuttings taken in summer. Keep plants well pruned, as they can become starchy and straggly, with a resulting loss of flavour. Allow 60cm/24 inches between plants, and watch out for powdery mildew in very hot weather.

HOW TO USE

Leaves can be picked at any time during the growing season for immediate use. Harvest plants after flowers have bloomed for drying, and hang these upside down.

Sage is a traditional ingredient of stuffing, and a delicious accompaniment to poultry dishes. It is also a classic bouquet garni mainstay. Leaves can also be brewed into a relaxing tea.

A sage tea can ease sore throats and gums, either drunk or as a mouthwash. It can also relieve indigestion and minor upset stomachs. Sage should not be taken to excess, as it can have harmful effects, and should not be taken as a medicine by pregnant women.

POSITION

SOIL TYPE

PROPAGATION

PARTS USED

USES

PESTS/DISEASES

ELDER

Sambucus Nigra

The lacy white flowers and delicate scent of the elder make it a familiar sight in hedgerows and meadows, and it has a history rich in folklore.

HISTORY

Elder has a strong folkloric tradition common to many cultures. Widely regarded as a 'cure-all', it features in many ancient herbal remedies. Species of elder have been used as medicines by Native Americans, the ancient Egyptians and throughout Europe. Once thought to have the power to protect against witches, held as sacred by traditional gypsy tribes and also associated with the Jewish Cabbala, it was also widely believed that cutting back an elder plant would bring bad luck.

CHARACTERISTICS

A hardy perennial shrub or tree, elder can, if left unchecked, reach a height of 10 m/30 feet and a spread of 2 m/8 feet, but most plants will be considerably smaller. Leaves are pointed, with a finely toothed edge. Elder is most recognisable by its flat, feathery clusters of tiny white-gold flowers, which appear in the early summer. Berries are small and black and grouped closely together.

GROWING TIPS

Elder is best grown from cuttings taken in autumn if hardwood or summer if softwood. A moist, well-drained soil with plenty of sun is ideal. Allow plenty of space around each plant to avoid crushing when full growth is reached. Pruning depends on your preferred use of elder.
If ornament and fragrance is you prime concern, plants should be pruned hard during winter.
If you require good crops of flowers or berries, a light pruning is recommended.

HOW TO USE

Flowers should be harvested once they have fully opened. The whole head should be dried. Collect berries when they are ripe.

Although parts of the plant are used for culinary purposes, the leaves and fruit should never be eaten raw.

The flowers can be used to flavour fruit desserts or summer drinks, while the berries can be mixed with other fruits for jams and preserves. Both flowers and berries are commonly used for wine.

A rinse of elder flower water can make a refreshing skin toner, while a decoction of fruits or flowers can relieve feverish complaints such as colds and flu.

COMFREY

Symphytum officinale

A well-established medicinal herb, comfrey is long-lived and adaptable. Its distinctive bell flowers make it a decorative, as well as useful, plant.

HISTORY

A native of Asia and Europe, although now widespread throughout temperate regions, comfrey has been a staple of the herbal medicine chest for centuries. During Mediaeval times, it was used so widely in medicine that it was regarded as a cure for almost any ailment. Its most famous application is as an aid to the setting of broken bones – hence its familiar name of 'knit-bone' – and recorded usage in this way dates back to the ancient Greeks.

CHARACTERISTICS

Comfrey is a hardy perennial that reaches around 60cm/24 inches in height, and half this in spread. Leaves are a rather dull, dark green in colour, and can grow to 20cm/8 inches long. They are veined, hairy, and singularly unattractive. This is made up for by the bell-shaped flowers, which range in colour from cream through red and purple, and which form in clusters. These flowers bloom from late spring through summer.

GROWING TIPS

Comfrey requires moist to wet soil and plenty of sunshine. Full sunlight is preferred, but partial shade will not be harmful. Seeds should be sown in autumn or spring, while cuttings can be transplanted or divided in spring or autumn. A single piece of root is all that is needed to grow a patch of comfrey, and as the plant is deep rooted, they establish well. Take care where you place them, as comfrey can easily take over a bed, and is difficult to remove when grown. Allow plenty of space around each plant – 1 square metre/40 square inches is recommended.

HOW TO USE

Young leaves should be picked in the spring or early summer, while roots should be gathered in autumn, after the plant has begun to die back. Always leave some root remaining, for next year's growth. Leaves should be stripped from stems as needed. They can be dried flat on racks.

Comfrey has been little used in cooking, and today its use for medicinal purposes is somewhat controversial, as some research suggests the plant may contain harmful elements in its raw state. For this reason, our suggestions for comfrey taken internally only include decoctions or infusions, which are considered safe, as the herb is diluted.

In tea form, comfrey can be taken to aid gastric inflammations or chest complaints. However, if in doubt about using comfrey in this way, there are other herbs with equally beneficial properties.

A comfrey poultice can be applied to broken bones, sprains, burns and bruises, and a comfrey root decoction can also be applied to stem the flow of bleeding from small wounds.

TYPES

POSITION

SOIL TYPE

PROPAGATION

PARTS USED

USES

Comfrey

Thyme

THYME

Thymus vulgaris

TYPES

POSITION

SOIL TYPE

PROPAGATION

PARTS USED

USES

PESTS/DISEASES

A beautifully fragrant and colourful plant, thyme is a delightful addition to any herb bed. The different varieties each have a subtle and distinctive flavour, making thyme as pleasing to the tastebuds, as it is to the eye.

HISTORY

One of the oldest-known herbs, thyme was in use at the time of the ancient Greeks, and probably dates back many years earlier. One of the many plants introduced to England by the Romans, thyme is a feature of many culinary recipes, as well as having a place in the herbal medicine cabinet. In addition, thyme has a part to play in folklore. It shares with other aromatic plants a pleasant association with death, in that the souls of the dead were thought to become one with the flowers. Indeed, the sweet smell of thyme has often been reported at reputedly haunted sites. Carrying thyme was also once popular with young women, as it supposedly helped to identify their true love!

CHARACTERISTICS

A low-growing (usually up to 30cm/12 inches in both height and spread) hardy perennial shrub, thyme has small, narrow leaves and clusters of tiny flowers in hues of pink and purple. Stems tend to look woody as they age, and plants can become straggly if not kept trim.

GROWING TIPS

Certain species of thyme can be planted in seed form in spring, although most varieties grow best from cuttings in spring and summer. Summer or autumn is best for dividing plants. Thyme thrives in relatively poor soil; in fact a gravelly, stony soil is ideal, as this helps drainage – important as thyme grows poorly in over-wet ground. Thyme requires full sunlight, although some shade is acceptable. Thyme is also an ideal herb to grow in pots indoors, kept on a south-facing windowsill. Groups of plants should be spaced around 30cm/12 inches apart. As thyme thrives best in a warm, sunny environment, they will need care and protection during the winter months.

HOW TO USE

During the growing season, stem tips should be snipped in the mornings for immediate use. If harvesting larger quantities for drying, cut the whole plant back to around 5cm/2 inches above the ground. This should be done before the plant blooms. Sprigs of thyme can be frozen on trays, or whole branches can be dried by hanging in paper sacks. They can also be dried by microwave.

Thyme can be used in cookery to accompany almost any dish. It is a classic ingredient of a bouquet garni for inclusion in soups and casseroles, enhances the flavour of most meat and poultry dishes, and can be combined with oils and vinegars for delicious marinades.

Medicinally, thyme can be infused to aid stomach complaints, and its antiseptic properties make it ideal as a mouthwash or gargle, or even for cleaning small scrapes and grazes. An infusion of thyme is also thought to alleviate the effects of drinking too much alcohol, as Nicholas Culpeper recorded in his directory.

TYPES

POSITION

SOIL TYPE

PROPAGATION

PARTS USED

USES

MULLEIN

Verbascum thapsus

This tall, attractive plant will make a striking and decorative addition to a herb garden, although it can easily take over if allowed to self-sow.

HISTORY

Used as a medicinal plant since ancient times, particularly for respiratory complaints, mullein is a popular addition to cosmetic treatments today.

CHARACTERISTICS

A hardy biennial, mullein is easily recognisable by its long pointed leaves topped by a crown of deep yellow flowers. Both sides of the leaves are covered with a soft, white fur. A long stem grows every other year – smaller stems grow in alternate years.

GROWING TIPS

Mullein should be planted from seed in spring or autumn, or by root cuttings in winter. Full sun is preferred, and a dry, well-drained soil is ideal. Mullein self-sows extremely easily, so will need to be thinned regularly.

HOW TO USE

Whole plants should be harvested as the plant is flowering. Leaves and flowers can be dried, and the flowers can also be used fresh, or frozen.

Mullein leaves and flowers are both said to be effective in treating respiratory ailments when brewed in a decoction. The flowers are considered particularly effective in relieving bronchitis.

Mullein can also be mixed with other herbs for an effective hair cleanser.

The seeds of Mullein are toxic, and should never be taken internally.

GINGER

Zingiber officinale

This much-prized spice has held its popular position for centuries. Traditionally used in both cookery and medicine, the attractive flowers of the ginger plant also make it a decorative addition to any garden.

HISTORY

Cultivated throughout both the East and West, ginger's importance was such that it was once recorded as a taxable item by the Romans. Featuring strongly in many Chinese herbal remedies, as well as in Oriental cookery, ginger has also been used for centuries as a medicinal aid in western countries.

CHARACTERISTICS

A tender perennial, the gnarly, bulbous ginger root produces a single stalk of narrow stemless leaves, followed in summer by pale green flowers that gradually reach a dark purple colour towards the edges. A ginger plant can reach a height of 1.5 m/60 inches. The flavour of ginger is sharp and spicy, and the taste becomes hotter when the root is dried.

GROWING TIPS

Ginger thrives in a tropical climate, so needs a degree of humidity. If your weather conditions are particularly cool, you may be better off growing ginger in a greenhouse. Soil should be moist and well-drained, and full sunshine is better in temperate climates. Divide plants in late spring for best growth, and allow a growing period of ten months for maximum effect.

HOW TO USE

The root part of the ginger used is known as the rhizome, and this can be harvested at any time during the growing season. For drying, it is best to wait until the plant is dormant. Ginger root can be stored in a cool dry place for up to three months, or preserved in brine or vinegar.

Ginger features in many Chinese and Japanese dishes, and is also popular in curries, pickles and chutneys. Dried, ground ginger is also delicious in cakes and desserts.

Medicinally, ginger is used to relieve stomach upsets and nausea, menstrual cramps and as a digestive aid. It is also believed to relieve the symptoms of food poisoning. As with garlic, ginger is also held to aid the reduction of cholesterol levels and high blood pressure.

TYPES

POSITION

SOIL TYPE

PROPAGATION

PARTS USED

USES

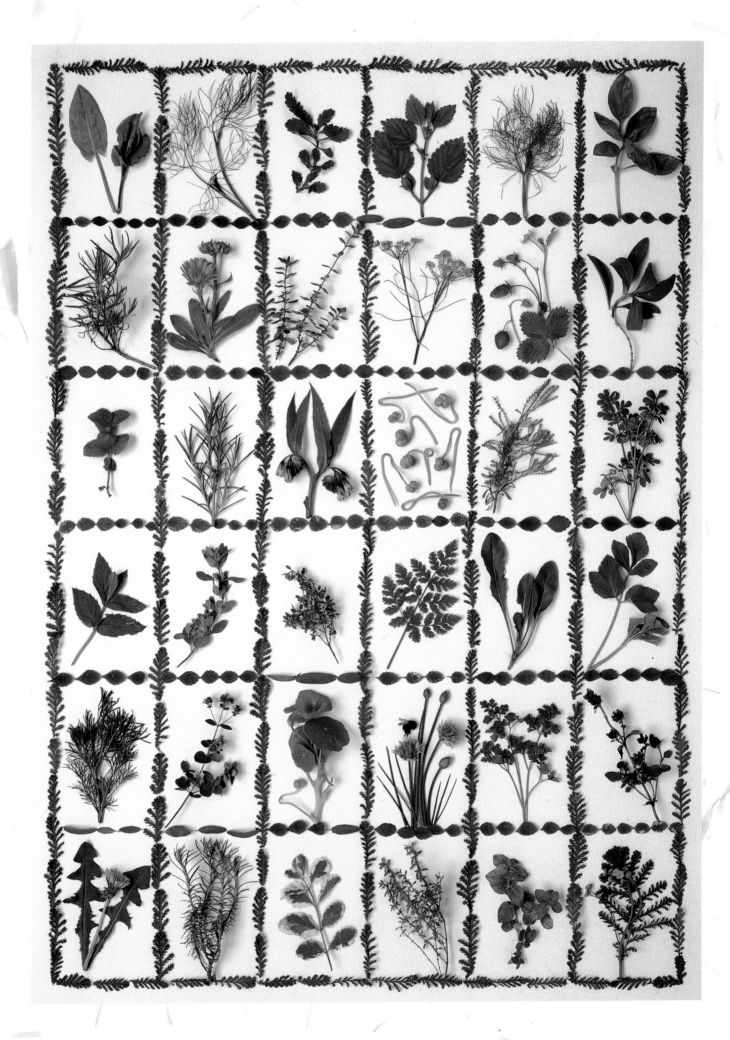

GROWING HERBS

In this section we will look at all aspects of the planning and maintenance of a healthy herb garden – from planning your garden design, through choosing your plants to caring for them at each stage of their development.

Contents

Growing your own Herbs

INTRODUCTION

For centuries, the growing of herbs for home use was a common practice. Specially designed and cultivated herb gardens, famed as much for their fragrance as for the variety of herbs they contained, were almost *de rigeur* amongst those who could afford them, whilst those who had to rely on the produce of their gardens for the bulk of their sustenance would usually grow a handful of the more common herbs among their vegetables.

Herb border with brick edge. Chives, feverfew.

In more recent times, the use of fresh herbs began to decline. As modern medicines ousted herbal remedies from their traditional place in the treatment of illness and pains, so too the growing availability and convenience of dried and preserved seasonings reduced the requirement for fresh herbs.

Window box with parsley, sage, thyme, fennel.

partially responsible. So too is the increased health-consciousness that has become widespread over recent years, with more people turning to fresh ingredients and

Today the tide has turned once more, and the growing of herbs at home has become more and more popular. Renewed interest in the benefits of traditional herbal remedies is

home-cooked meals rather than convenience foods.

Yet there is more to the current popularity of herbs than this. Those who make the decision to grow their own herbs either for seasonings or home remedies also rediscover the sheer delight of herbs in their own right. Many herbs have beautiful flowers, and look wonderful in full bloom, while others have a delightful aroma which adds an extra touch to any garden or home.

And the beauty of herbs is that they can be grown anywhere. A selection of herbs grown in pots indoors can be just as delightful as a series of beds and borders in a garden. With careful planning, and a little imagination, you can create a beautiful herb garden anywhere, regardless of the space you have available.

In this section we will be looking at the various options for planting herbs, from beds and borders to containers. By following the advice and instructions on buying, growing, propagation and care, you will soon be ready to create your own herb garden.

Herb pot with rosemary, bay, tarragon and parsley.

Country herbal arrangement.

Planning your Garden

The directory at the beginning of this book will give you much useful advice on the properties and requirements of the most popular herbs, and it is important to ensure that the herbs you select are suitable for where you have chosen to plant them.

Planning a herb garden is one of the most satisfying stages for even the most experienced of gardeners, and even those with little knowledge of growing can take heart from the fact that herbs are some of the easiest plants to cultivate.

In general, most herbs, having originated in the warmer, Mediterranean climate, require at least five or six hours of sunlight a day, although there are some which thrive in shadier areas of the garden. Again, the herb directory will tell you which these are. In areas where colder weather is more common, herbs can still be grown successfully, although they will need a little more nurturing, in the form of windbreaks or perhaps a glass frame.

A simple arrangement of herb pots can be effective.

If possible, plant your herbs close to the house. Not only will you have more opportunity to enjoy their fragrance, this also places them conveniently to hand when you wish to gather them.

For maximum benefit, do not restrict your herb garden simply to those you know you will use the most. Try to incorporate some herbs for their other properties, rather than just their usefulness. Include some that simply look or smell beautiful, as well as a few that you are unfamiliar with, and wish to learn more about.

Herbs generally fall into two categories, annual and perennial, so when designing your herb garden, try to ensure that the two are kept separate. Annuals need to be cleared out at the end of their season, and you run the risk of disturbing your ongoing plants if you have them growing too closely together.

Your herb garden design can take many forms, and it is valuable to draw up a scale plan to give you a true idea of the space you have available. Check your directory for the potential height and growth spread of your proposed herbs, as this will allow you to determine which herbs can be planted together, and which would thrive better in separate beds. The last thing you want is for a fast growing and spreading plant to overrun its companions.

Once you have determined the plants that are suitable for the area you have chosen, you need to decide whether you would prefer a formal arrangement, as found in many stately homes and gardens, or a more random, cottage garden effect.

An important consideration is the style of the rest of your garden. If in general your garden is unplanned, with plants growing haphazardly, a formal knot garden may look out of place, for example, while an informal, rambling bed of herbs may strike a discordant note if everything else in your garden is meticulously planned. However, personal preference should be your guide.

For a formal garden you may wish to group your plants according to colour, size or texture. If combining, it is generally best to

A herb garden can be a soothing and attractive place to relax.

Formal, Gothic-style herb garden with sage.

place taller plants to the back when planning a border – or in the middle if you choose an enclosed bed – and work down in scale. If you are planning several beds, each could contain a very different style, perhaps grouped by colour. Alternatively, if you are planning just one bed, you can separate each group of herbs by using bricks, or plants such as dwarf lavender, which grows low to the ground. This was the method favoured by the Elizabethans for their knot gardens.

A coloured theme can have dramatic effects.

However you choose to plant your garden, consider carefully the appearance of each plant in flower. Exciting visual effects can be achieved by placing together herbs of vivid, contrasting tones, while if a riot of colour is not your preference, choose herbs with more

muted, complementary hues.

Lack of space in your garden, or even the lack of a garden at all need not stand in the way of creating your own herb garden. A few pots on a terrace or patio, or even your windowsill can be marvellously effective.

Even gardens on such a small scale need careful planning - perhaps even more so - as every part of the container should be used to maximum effect, and your choice of herbs, both in terms of their size and colour, as well as their suitability for growing in pots, is particularly important.

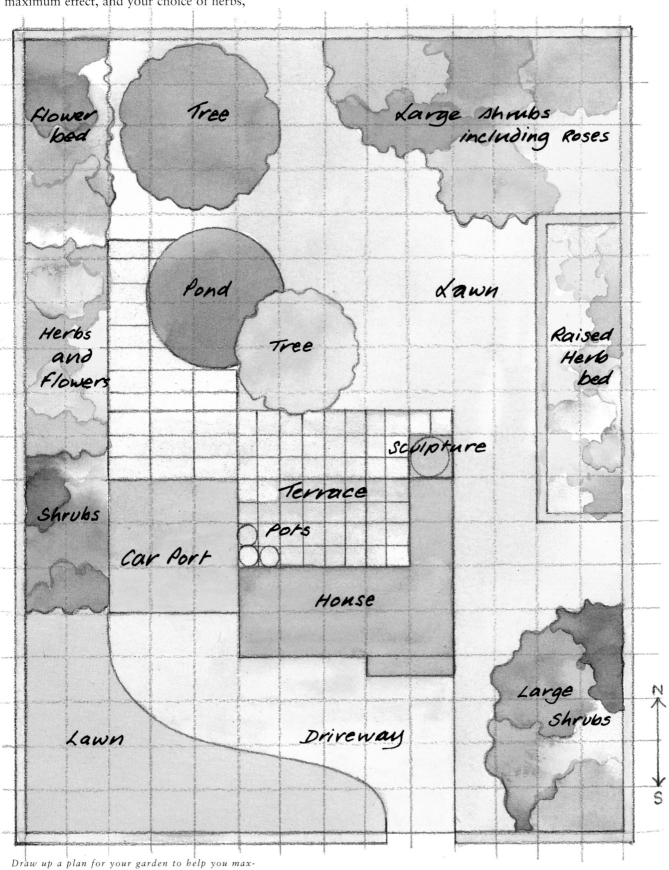

Flower bed

Tree

Large Shrubs including Roses

Pond

Lawn

Tree

Herbs and Flowers

Raised Herb bed

Sculpture

Terrace

Shrubs

Pots

Car Port

House

Lawn

Driveway

Large Shrubs

N

S

Draw up a plan for your garden to help you maximise the effect of your design.

Formal Garden Design

A good design lies at the heart of your herb garden, and traditionally such gardens have followed very formal, geometric patterns. The shape or pattern you choose will be largely governed by the space you have allocated for your herb bed, and what elements your garden already contains.

Do you have a pathway, for example? A simple herb border can look very effective alongside an existing path. Use any pathway as a design guide to help you form your beds. If you are growing herbs in a border against a hedge or fence, a cascade effect, with the tallest plants at the back, can also be very eye-catching.

Will your herb bed be raised, or at ground level? Take a good look around your garden, and experiment with designs to determine which existing features may enhance your herb selection.

A central feature in the garden makes a good starting point for your design.

A wall makes an appealing, and protective, background to a border.

FORMAL BEDS

One of the most effective formal bed designs is based around a series of repeated, geometric shapes. These can be squares, for a chess board effect; a circle divided into wedges around a central feature; a diamond or any other pattern you desire. A line of bricks makes an ideal dividing line between your herb groups.

Before beginning, measure your chosen plot, and draw a scale plan of your desired pat-tern. When you begin marking the bed out on the ground, use rope to indicate any paths or dividing lines between beds. It is always a good idea to study this marked-out design very carefully before you begin to work on your garden. This will help you visualise the finished bed from various angles – see what it looks like from an upstairs window, or check that there is space around the bed to walk around and that the paths are easily negotiable. If you are creating or using existing pathways, make sure these will be clearly defined. The same applies if

Place taller plants at the back of your border for an attractive tiered look.

Growing Herbs in Containers

Where space in your garden is restricted, or your soil is not suitable for growing, many herbs can be successfully grown in containers. These could be pots, tubs or window boxes which have the advantage of being moveable, so plants can be placed in sunnier parts of your garden if required. Alternatively your container could take the form of a raised bed. Even unusual objects such as wheelbarrows can be transformed into a stunning herb bed.

Hanging baskets are ideal for herbal arrangements if space is limited.

For all containers, you should first obtain a suitable compost for your herbs. Rather than place herbs directly into the container, it is better to place them in smaller pots first. In some cases you may have brought herb plants already potted, or you may have grown plants from seed, or taken cuttings from existing plants. Make holes for these smaller pots, then place them into the container, covering the pot rim with peat or gravel across the container. This makes it easier should you wish to replace one of the herbs, as the pot can simply be dug out and another put in its place. With the peat or gravel smoothed over once more, your container garden will seem unchanged, and your other plants will not have been disturbed.

Container gardens require a good deal of care, and watering is essential, particularly in warmer weather. When using pots or other moveable containers, try to ensure that your plants get plenty of light – most plants require around five to six hours of sunshine per day.

A window box allows you to appreciate the aroma and appearance of your herbs while indoors.

If your garden soil is unsuitable for growing herbs, but you would prefer a more permanent container arrangement, you can easily build a raised bed. These can be made to any shape or size, and are especially appealing built from red bricks or stone. As with other containers, they require a suitable compost, and attention. An advantage of a raised bed is that the fragrance of the herbs is brought even closer, and they are also easier for the elderly or infirm to maintain, as the strain of bending to attend to the bed is greatly reduced.

Herbs can be grown in pots on raised surfaces for ease of access.

Even the most unusual objects make distinctive herb containers.

Preparing Herb Beds

CLEARING THE GROUND

Once you have decided upon the style of your herb garden, it is time to mark out the layout and break ground. We have previously advised that you lay out the pattern with rope to study its position and convenience, but now you must lay out your design exactly.

Mark out your bed using stakes and rope or a garden hose.

The best way to lay out a straight-edged design is to measure your pattern carefully, then set stakes at each corner. Simply stretch string or twine between each post and you

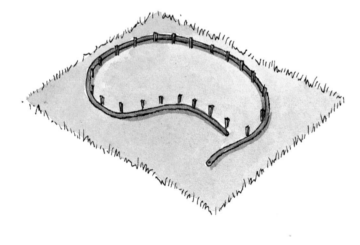

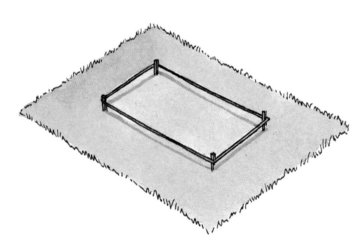

have easy-to-follow lines. For curved lines you can use either rope or a garden hose to mark your lines. Secure into place with wooden stakes.

If you are setting your bed in a lawned area, you will have to remove the grass first. Turf can either be removed in chunks, or stripped and rolled. Use your spade to score a chunk of turf to remove - watch the size, as you need to be able to lift the chunk on the spade. Then deepen your score line to about a spade's depth along each edge, and dig out the chunk of earth. Once you have removed the first piece of turf, the rest will be easier.

Stripping and rolling is easier than it sounds, as you simply use your spade to mark strips along the space to be cleared, loosen these strips, again to about a spade's depth, then carefully roll up the turf strip. If you are stripping a larger area you can hire a special machine.

An alternative option if you are in no hurry to begin planting is to simply cover your area of lawn with 3–5 cm/1–2 inches of black polythene or newspapers. Cover this with 10–15 cm/4–6 inches of straw or chipped bark, and water thoroughly. Now you must leave this to mulch for a year, when you can plant your herbs into the mulched bed.

TENDING YOUR SOIL

Once you have cleared your lawn, or if you are planting in an existing bed, you will probably need to improve your soil. Soil types vary considerably between regions, ranging from sandy and dry to sticky clay, but whatever your soil type there is little doubt that increasing its organic content will be highly beneficial. Organic additives can take the form of leaf mould, grass clippings, peelings and manure. As most herbs grow quite happily in average soil, you will find that simply improving the organic content will provide an adequate soil for them to thrive in.

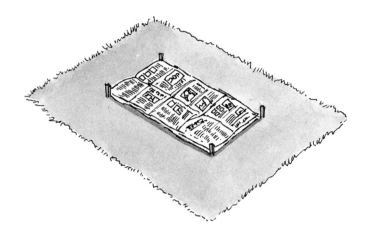

Adding compost also improves the aeration and drainage of your soil. Permanently damp soil will not help your herbs to flourish, so ensuring that the water drains correctly is very important. The easiest way to check this is to simply water your chosen patch of ground, and watch what happens. If the water sits on the surface, the chances are that your soil contains too much clay. If on the following day only the first inch or so of the soil is damp, then it is probably too sandy. The most effective way to improve aeration and drainage is to dig over your ground to a reasonable depth - the depth of your garden spade is ideal. Dig into this about 15cm/6 inches of compost. This will improve the drainage in clay-based soils, and help sandy soils to hold moisture.

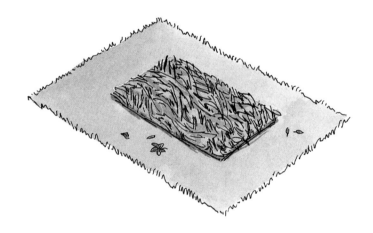

You have now chosen your garden design and the varieties of herbs to place in it, and have prepared your ground for planting. The next decision you must make is whether to grow your herbs from seed, or to choose grown plants or cuttings.

If you are in no hurry, mulching your bed for one year will prepare the soil.

Checking the soil
type around your
plants.

Buying Herbs

The quickest and easiest way to start your garden is by buying herbs, rather than taking cuttings or growing your own herbs from seed. You will find a wide variety of herbs available at garden centres or nurseries, and these are generally available at various stages of maturity.

In general, you will always do best by buying from a reputable nursery or garden centre, and there are some useful guidelines for choosing your plants. In the introduction

we looked at the confusion that can arise from mistaking one plant or variety for another, so always ensure that you know the full botanical names of the plants you require to avoid confusion.

Another handy tip is to always check the labelling of your plant. It is not unheard of for labels to be misplaced, or for plants to be labelled incorrectly, so you may end up with a different plant than you had thought. If you have planned your garden carefully, a

A good nursery will allow plenty of room for plants to thrive.

If you have several plant suppliers to choose from, visit each of them to see the environment the plants are kept in. Plants that are ragged or cramped closely together are less likely to thrive, so always choose somehwere that allows plenty of space for the plants to grow.

It is not necessary to limit yourself to large, commercial nurseries, however. Keep an eye out for small garden shops or market stalls which often stock plants at a fraction of the price of their larger competitors. Country fairs and fêtes can also be excellent places to pick up plant bargains.

As a general guide, avoid buying plants that are in flower, and check that the colour of the plant is strong and healthy. Look for any signs of disease or insects, and do not choose plants that have roots escaping from the base of their containers, as this means that they have remained potted for rather too long.

Markets are excellent places to find herb bargains.

rogue herb may ruin the effect. If you are unsure, leave your purchase until you can check with your herb guide.

Always check labels carefully when buying herbs.

Growing from Seed

Herbs can be grown from seed both indoors or outdoors. Annuals are usually the easiest and quickest herbs to grow from seed, and your seedlings should begin to appear within a few days.

If you choose to sow outdoors, your bed must be free from weeds and stones, and the soil needs to be raked thoroughly until it is fine and crumbly. Wait at least until the warmer days of spring before planting, to avoid the danger of frost, and allow the sun to warm the soil well before beginning.

Planting indoors gives you the advantage of starting your seeds earlier in the year, so you will have seedlings ready for transplanting once the warmer weather has arrived. If you have never grown plants from seed before, we would recommend using peat blocks, as these can be transplanted to the garden as they are, without disturbing the delicate herb roots. When using trays or pots, any good potting soil is suitable, but remember to keep the soil evenly moist. Fill your container to about 12 mm/½ inch from the top, being careful not to pack the soil too firmly, as plant roots need some space to

take hold. Plant your seeds according to the instructions on the packet, then cover with a fine layer of soil. Always ensure that you label each variety of herb correctly.

Stand your container on a waterproof tray, and water your seeds daily. For best results cover the pots with a piece of glass or plastic until the seedlings have begun to appear. Then transfer the pots to a sunny windowsill. Once the seedlings have taken root you will need to thin them to give the remaining plants room to develop fully. Allow about 1 inch of soil around each root.

Once your plants have reached a height of several inches, and are growing strong and healthy, you should allow them to acclimatise to conditions out of doors before transplanting them to your herb bed. Place them by an open window, or outside in the sun for a few hours each day, but do bring them in at night. Continue this for three or four days, when your young plants will be ready for transplanting into their new home.

Healthy seedling. *Sparse seedling.* *Cover seeded trays or pots with plastic or glass.*

Space seeds evenly when sowing.

Propagation

While annuals are quick and easy to grow from seed, perennial herbs and shrubs are best grown from shoots or cuttings. In general, spring is the best time of year for this, although there are some exceptions such as rosemary which take root more successfully from cuttings taken in late summer.

If taking cuttings, choose a stem with at least five leaves. Make an angled cut, and remove the stem. Remove the two bottom leaves from the stem, and leave the end to dry for around four hours. Place the stem gently but firmly in a soil filled pot, and repeat for any other cuttings. Keep your cuttings in a cool, shady spot, and cover with a plastic sheet to encourage growth. When new green leaves begin to appear, your cutting has been successful, and your plants are ready to be transplanted. For plants with trailing stems, the best method of propagation is by layering and division. Take a long stem from your plant, and lay it along the soil. Pin it gently to the soil, taking care to ensure it remains

Take rosemary cuttings during late summer.

connected to the parent plant. Watch this stem carefully, and you will see new roots beginning to grow after a few days where the stem touches the soil. Wait until these roots have become well established, then cut the stem connecting the new plant and its parent. The young plant is now ready to be transplanted to its new home.

TIPS

Before propagation, do ensure that you are using the correct method for each plant.

Although a cutting or division may establish if taken at a different time of the year, try to propagate during the recommended times of the year, to give your herb the best chance of survival.

Even though you have followed all the guidelines, you may find that some, or even all, of your propagated plants have not established. Do not be discouraged, as even in the best conditions, success is not guaranteed every time.

Choose stems with at least 5 leaves, and make angled cuts.

Preparing pots and trays for herb cuttings.

Cuttings should be covered with plastic to encourage growth.

Transplanting

Once you have chosen your herbs and brought them home, or your seedlings or cuttings are strong enough to be moved, you are ready to transplant them into your prepared bed. Direct sunlight can have a detrimental effect on newly transplanted herbs, and they make take several days to recover, so try to do your planting either on a cloudy day, during the early hours of the morning or later in the afternoon when the sun is not so strong. Excessive sunlight can be detrimental to the health of young plants, particularly if they are being unsettled. Once you have dug the holes for your plants, water them well - but be careful not to overwater – so the newcomers have an immediate supply of moisture.

Transplanted herbs can be placed directly into your bed.

If your plants or seedlings are in standard pots, ensure that you keep the maximum amount of soil around the roots when you remove them from the pots. Cup your hand over the top of the pot, and gently tip the pot upside down. The roots, together with much of the soil, should slide out quite easily. If they do not, try gently loosening the soil around the edge of the pot before tipping. Try not to shake the pot too vigorously – this could damage the roots, as well as showering you with loose soil if the plant suddenly comes free. If roots are tangled around the outside of the pot, gently loosen these before removing the plant, to avoid tearing them.

If you wish to contain the roots of your plant, so that they do not spread too widely and possibly affect neighbouring herbs, you can transplant the herb into a pot already dug into the ground. This will also aid removal should you wish to reposition plants at a later date.

Once you have removed the plant, place it so that the roots are only just below ground level, and water gently. Add more soil to the hole, and pack in quite firmly to allow the roots to take a good hold. Then water them again. Watch your new plants carefully, and continue watering frequently until you see new leaves appear. Once these have arrived you will know that your plants have become well established.

Herbs can be planted into a pot dug into the soil to contain roots.

Maintainting your Herb Garden

Once your seedlings or transplanted herbs have taken hold, the care and time they need to keep them thriving is minimal, but important. Between now and harvest time, your tasks will be simply thinning, weeding, watering and perhaps mulching. With all the hard work you have put into planning, growing or cutting, you can now watch and enjoy as your herb garden begins to flourish.

THINNING

Once young herbs have grown two sets of leaves, you will need to thin them to ensure that your herbs have enough space to grow. The directory at the beginning of the book provides details of how much space to allow for each of the most popular herbs. Thinning gives each plant room to gain the food, water and sunlight they need. It may seem callous to remove healthy plants to give space to those remaining, but overcrowding is a sure way to an under-nourished herb bed.

The most effective way to thin your herbs is simply to pull the extra plants, together with their roots, from the soil. Alternatively you can cut the plants just below ground level. Always ensure that you have removed the roots of these extra plants, as any material remaining can rot, and spread disease to your remaining herbs. If you leave thinning for too long, the roots of the herbs may become intertwined, making removal of unwanted plants much harder.

WATERING

Once your plants are thinned to your satisfaction, and the individual needs of each herb, you will need to keep a careful eye on the water supply of your herb garden. From your preparations, you should have an idea of the type of soil you have, and now you should begin to develop an awareness of how quickly this soil dries out, which will determine the frequency of watering necessary. It is a good idea in these early stages to check your beds once a day, or at least every other day once plants are well established. Remember that you will need to water more frequently in summer than in autumn, when most herbs are dormant.

Remember also to water more than just the surface of your beds. To develop healthy, deep roots, your herbs need plenty of water – the soil should be moist to around 20cm deep. A sprinkler hose set to a timer is a good way of ensuring your plants get adequate water, but a watering can or ordinary hose is sufficient as long as you are thorough. If you have limited time, it is far better to give your beds a good deep watering every few days, rather than rushing and merely sprinkling the surface of the soil on a daily basis.

The best time for watering your plants is early in the morning. This allows the soil plenty of time to absorb the moisture before it evaporates as the day grows warmer. Plants left damp overnight are more prone to fungal diseases, so avoid watering too late in the day.

WEEDING

With effective care and attention, your herb garden should be thriving. Unfortunately, it is more than likely that you will also begin to notice some unwelcome guests – weeds. Regular weeding not only ensures that your herbs do not have to compete for precious

space, but also keeps your garden looking beautiful.

Weeds can seem to grow at an alarming rate, so make sure you weed regularly. Try and avoid disturbing the soil too much as you remove weeds, as this minimises the opportunities for weed seeds deeper in the

Container herb
gardens will need
extra care and
attention to thrive.

ground to spring into life. Pull each weed out separately, rather than simply grabbing a handful. The task may take longer, but weeding in this way is ultimately more effective. You will find that no sooner has one batch of weeds been defeated that a new season will appear. However, by mid or late summer you will find that weeding is pretty much a thing of the past.

If the idea of fighting weeds every year is not something you find appealing, you do have an easy alternative – mulching. Mulching helps prevent the growth of weed seeds, and is also beneficial in that it helps retain water, which reduces the need for frequent watering. Woodchips, straw or shredded leaves are all good mulches. Grass clippings should only be used for annual herbs, as they release nitrogen as they rot. While this can provide extra nourishment for annuals, perennials will not benefit from this.

For plants that like cooler conditions, mulch when they are around 15 cm/6 inches tall, and mulch to just under half their height. For plants that prefer warmth, wait until late spring when the soil has had a chance to warm through, before mulching. Leave an area free of mulch around stems or sprays of leaves, otherwise you are handing out an open invitation to slugs and other pests.

CARING FOR CONTAINER GARDENS

As well as watering daily, you will also have to add an organic fertilizer around once a fortnight, as herbs in containers do not have access to the nutrients available in the soil of a garden bed. For plants kept in smaller pots on windowsills, ensure that you turn the pots every so often so that each side of your plant will benefit from the sun.

Following these simple, but vital, steps will ensure that your beds or containers will flourish, and by the end of your first season you should have a healthy, well-established herb garden. Useful, beautiful to look at and a fascinating and rewarding hobby, planning, creating and caring for your herb garden, be it a complicated formal design or simply one or two pots or tubs, will prove a delight for many years to come.

USING HERBS IN COOKERY

Herbs have been used for centuries to enhance the natural flavour of food, and today herb recipes feature in almost every cookery book on the market. Here we look at just a few ways that herbs can make a subtle difference to your meal times.

Contents

Using Herbs in Cookery

INTRODUCTION

The tradition of using herbs to flavour foods is nothing new. It is, in fact, almost as old as the human species itself. Archaeologists have found evidence which suggests that the earliest cooks used parts of certain plants to season and improve the flavour of particular foods. Mustard seed was chewed with meat, it seems, and the seeds of wild wheat and barley were sprinkled on other foods to add a nutty taste.

These herbs would, of course, have been found growing wild, and the cultivation of herbs for culinary and medicinal use came much later. In grand old gardens, a special section would be set aside for the growing of herbs, while in humbler plots herbs might be grown among other food plants. This delightful tradition is well worth continuing: what could be more satisfying than being able to pick fresh herbs from your own garden to add to the dishes for a summer lunch, or the evening meal? The aroma alone as you pick the herbs is the perfect appetizer.

Herbs make delicious ingredients in salads, dressings and oils.

The range of herbs, even for culinary purposes, is huge, and few of us nowadays will have either the space, time or inclination to grow all the varieties found in the traditional herb garden. Nevertheless, a small bed of the more common herbs – or just a selection of pots by the kitchen door, on a balcony or window sill will give your cooking a fresh and distinctive flavour.

COOKING WITH HERBS

Herbs used in cooking may be fresh, dried, or frozen (see Harvesting and Preserving on pages 145–9). Fresh herbs do not have the concentrated flavour of the dried variety but make up for this by being more aromatic – just try crushing a fresh leaf between your fingers and breathing in its glorious scent.

Fresh herbs can be used in cooked dishes (in which case, add them towards the end of the cooking time to retain their freshness of flavour). However, the best way to preserve their 'straight-from-the-garden' quality is, in

many cases, to use them in their natural state – raw. The traditional sprig of parsley or scattering of chives certainly looks attractive, but do consider using certain of the softer-leaved herbs as ingredients in their own right. Quantities of finely chopped mint combined with yogurt make the classic Greek tsatsiki – the perfect summer cooler – while whole basil leaves added to an ordinary green salad move this everyday accompaniment several rungs up the culinary ladder. Of course, there are certain herbs that are too tough in their raw state to be used in this way, such as rosemary or bay, and these are best added to cooked dishes.

The drying of herbs intensifies their flavour, and means that herbal flavourings can be made available throughout the year, and not just in the summer growing season. Dried herbs are used in cooked foods, and can transform the most basic of dishes into something delicious and memorable. Frozen herbs bridge the gap between the fresh and dried varieties, and make it

*A mortar and pestle
is a useful tool for
grinding or
crushing herbs.*

all-rounder in the kitchen and can do much
to enliven an otherwise bland sauce or bake,
the real trick for the creative cook is
to choose the herb that will best complement
and bring out the flavour of a particular
food. Tarragon, for example, is superb with
roast chicken, while fennel seems to have
been made for fish. The aromas and tastes of
certain herbs can also evoke the cuisine of a
particular country or region. Coriander, for
example, conjures up images of Greece and
the Middle East; basil, with its affinity with
tomatoes and pasta, recalls Italy; while sage,
often used to flavour fresh pork, pork
sausages or earthy vegetables such as broad
beans, brings echoes of the hearty farmhouse
cooking of Northern Europe. Since this is a
book about the many different uses of herbs,

possible for the cook to evoke memories of
summer even in the depths of winter. Even
after thawing, however, frozen herbs will not
give the same results as fresh ones in such
dishes as salads, where the herbs act as
ingredients rather than just flavourings.

Whatever form of herb you are using – fresh,
dried or frozen – it is important to know
which herbs have an affinity with which
foods. While the standard 'mixed herbs'
product of the supermarket shelf is a good

*Mint is one of the
most popular
culinary herbs.
Apple mint has a
particularly
delicious flavour.*

*Herbs bring a
distinctive flavour
to any dish.*

the suggestions that follow are not recipes in
the expected sense – for that is the province
of a cookery book – but rather ideas that
will complement those dishes that you do
cook and bring all the delicious aromas and
tastes of culinary herbs to your table.

Grow parsley
close to your
house for
accessible fresh
herbs.

Seasonings and Garnishes

Here are some quick and easy ways to bring the delicious flavour of herbs to your cooking, and to give your dishes visual appeal, too.

BOUQUET GARNI

This method of flavouring food comes from classic French cuisine. Bouquet garni is best used in 'wet' recipes such as stocks, soups, stews, or poached vegetables, fish or meat, in which the cooking liquid absorbs the flavour of the herbs which then soaks into the ingredients. Two or three sprigs of fresh parsley, along with a single sprig or leaf of two or three other herbs, provides the basis of a bouquet garni. Experiment and find the combinations you like best for different foods.

Ground herbs make delicious salt-free seasonings.

INGREDIENTS
Kitchen twine or strong sewing thread
One of the following combinations of fresh herbs:
parsley, bay, sage
parsley, mint, chives
parsley, fennel, thyme, bay
parsley, tarragon, bay, chives
parsley, lemon thyme, bay, savoury
parsley, lovage, marjoram, bay
parsley, rosemary, sage
thyme, rosemary, oregano, bay
fennel, dill, bay

Tie the herbs together securely at the stalk end with the twine or thread. Immerse in the cooking liquid. Remove before serving.

SALTLESS SEASONING
Too much salt in our food is not considered good for health, so here is a salt-free seasoning mix which you can use instead. Having a pre-prepared quantity on hand means that you can quickly season a vinaigrette or some steamed vegetables without having to spend extra time slicing and chopping. Keep your seasoning in a shaker with large holes in the lid – an old salt canister or spice jar, thoroughly washed and dried, will do. Whatever you use, it should have a cap to keep the mixture airtight; alternatively, seal with clingfilm.

INGREDIENTS

50g/2 oz dried onion flakes
50g/2oz dried dill leaves
3 tablespoons sesame seeds, lightly toasted
1 tablespoon dried thyme
2 teaspoons dried oregano
2 teaspoons celery seeds
2 teaspoons dried lemon peel
1 teaspoon paprika
$1/2$ teaspoon garlic powder
$1/2$ teaspoon freshly ground black pepper

Grind all the ingredients together in a mortar and pestle or a coffee grinder. Place in a shaker and cap or seal tightly.

*Fresh Bouquet
Garni*

LAVENDER SUGAR

Store two or three dried heads of lavender in an airtight jar of caster sugar. This will scent the sugar beautifully. The sugar may be used sparingly in delicately flavoured dishes, such as simple sponge cakes, custards or ice cream.

CRYSTALLIZED LEAVES AND FLOWERS

For a pretty and edible decoration, crystallize mint leaves or borage flowers using this quick method. Whisk an egg white until it is very frothy. Then paint the leaves and flowers with egg white, and dip into caster sugar, which will cling to the egg white. Place on a wire tray and leave to dry.

Herbs Oils and Vinegars

The addition of a few well-chosen herbs can turn an ordinary culinary oil or vinegar into a gourmet item. Suitably trimmed and wrapped, home-made herb-flavoured oils and vinegars can make original, and delicious, gifts.

FLAVOURED OILS

Herb-flavoured oils can be used in marinades or vinaigrettes, brushed over meat or fish prior to grilling, or drizzled, Italian-style, over chunky toasted slices of baguette. Virgin olive oil or light sesame oil are best for this purpose, but other 'healthy' oils, such as sunflower or walnut, work well, too. Don't forget to label your oils so that you know what the bottles contain. Adding a fresh herb sprig to the oil before finally sealing makes an attractive touch, and intensifies the flavour.

INGREDIENTS
600ml/1 pint oil of your choice
6 tablespoons of chopped herbs in one of the following combinations:
basil, lemon thyme, rosemary
thyme, rosemary, shallots
basil, lemon thyme, chives, burnet, garlic
tarragon, lemon balm, green peppercorns
dill leaves, dill seeds, burnet, garlic

Use a mortar and pestle to pound the herbs to a paste. Add a few drops of the oil and stir to a cream, then slowly add the remaining oil. Pour the mixture into a clean, dry jar, cover and leave to steep for two weeks, shaking or stirring once or twice a day. Strain into a clean bottle, seal, label and store.

Herb flavoured oils make ideal marinades or dressings.

HERB VINEGARS

The addition of a herb vinegar will give an
instant lift to an ordinary vinaigrette, but try
using it in other ways, too. Stews, soups and
sauces all benefit from a splash of herb
vinegar towards the end of the cooking time,
and it can also replace some or all of the
wine called for in a recipe. The delicate
herbal flavour will be ruined if you use one
of the brash malt vinegars, though; opt
instead for a good-quality white wine or
cider vinegar.

INGREDIENTS
600ml/1 pint white wine or cider vinegar
A good quantity of herbs such as basil,
tarragon, bay leaves, thyme or mint

There is no need to chop or pound the herbs
– just pack the fresh leaves straight into a jar,
pour over the vinegar, cover, and leave to
steep on a sunny windowsill for two weeks,
shaking once or twice a day. Strain into a
clean bottle, add a fresh herb sprig if you
wish, seal, and store in a cool, dark place.
Experiment with combinations of
different herbs, too.

Herbal vinegars
can be used to
replace wine in
recipes for a deli-
cious flavour.

Sauces and Spreads

An aromatic herb butter, bringing with it all the scents of a summer garden, or a homemade herb sauce, can instantly transform the humblest and most plainly cooked of foods into something really special, and to end the meal, what could be more memorable that a selection of savoury biscuits served with a homemade herb cheese?

Creamy cheeses can be enlivened by adding herbs

HERB BUTTER

Parsley is the herb most commonly used in herb butters, but there are plenty of other alternatives. Try basil, mint, tarragon, or a combination of different herbs. You will need to choose carefully, however, because some herbs are not suitable for this purpose. Rosemary, for example, is too strong in flavour and coarse in texture to combine successfully with the smoothness and delicacy of the butter. Choose those herbs, too, that will best complement the food with which you are going to serve them. Mint butter melting over new potatoes is one excellent example of a perfect partnership.

Many herbs can be combined with butter to complement your dishes.

INGREDIENTS
100g/4oz unsalted butter
4-5 tablespoons of your chosen herb
1 teaspoon lemon juice

If the butter is too hard to work, leave it at room temperature to soften. Mash it with a

fork, working in the lemon juice, and then the herbs. Make sure all the ingredients are thoroughly combined. Spread on a saucer and place in the refrigerator to harden, then cut into cubes and arrange on a butter dish, or place on cooked foods just before serving.

HERB AND GARLIC CHEESE

This is an extremely easy way to transform an ordinary creamy cheese into a gourmet item, at a fraction of the price of the ready-made product. You can use full-fat cream cheese, curd cheese, or sieved cottage cheese but, if you opt for the latter, you will need to add 3 tablespoons of double cream to achieve the right consistency. As with herb butter, delicately flavoured herbs with fairly soft leaves, such as chives, chervil or parsley, are best for herb cheese.

INGREDIENTS
225g/8oz cream or curd cheese, or sieved cottage cheese
2-3 tablespoons finely chopped fresh herbs
1/2 clove finely chopped garlic

Work the garlic and herbs into the cheese with a fork, until all the ingredients are well combined. Form into a round, place on a dish, cover with clingfilm, and refrigerate before serving.

Herbal cheeses also make unusual gifts.

Summer Coolers

The leaves and flowers of herbs seem to embody the essence of summer, and there are numerous refreshing drinks containing herbs to cool you down on those sweltering mid-summer days. If you like the recipes offered here, you can go on to create your own delicious herb drinks, such as herb-flavoured fruit punches or creamy milk shakes.

MINTY LEMONADE

Homemade lemonade offers a completely different culinary experience from the fizzy and highly sweetened commercial drink of the same name. The addition of mint makes this recipe particularly refreshing. Try to use organically grown – or at least unwaxed – fruit for this recipe.

INGREDIENTS

3 lemons, plus extra juice to taste if needed
1 orange
250g/8oz honey, or more to taste
50g/2oz finely chopped fresh mint leaves
50g/2oz finely fresh lemon balm leaves
300ml/10fl. oz boiling water
1 litre/4 pints cold water
Sprigs of fresh mint and lemon balm, to decorate

Decorative ice cubes refresh any summer drink.

Peel the rind from the lemons and orange , being sure to remove any of the bitter white pith. Set aside while you squeeze out the juice. In a large heat-proof jug or bowl, combine the peel, honey and chopped herbs. Pour on the boiling water, and stir until the honey is blended in well. Allow to steep for 30 minutes. Then add the lemon and orange juice. Pour into a clean jug and add the cold water. Add extra honey and lemon juice to taste, as required. Chill for one hour. Pour into tumblers over ice cubes, and decorate with the herb sprigs.

ICED MINT TEA

Made in large quantities, this is the perfect drink for a summer garden party. Reduce the quantities proportionately if you are catering for a smaller occasion. The addition of sparkling soda water creates a very different beverage from the usual mint tea.

INGREDIENTS
(TO MAKE APPROXIMATELY 6 LITRES/ 1 1/4 GALLONS)
3 litres/120fl. oz strong tea
1.5 litres/60fl. oz soda water
750g/1 1/2 lb caster sugar
450ml/15fl. oz lemon juice
mint sprigs and ice, to serve
slices of lemon and orange, to decorate (optional)

Pour the tea into a large bowl or enamelled saucepan, add the sugar and leave to cool. Stir in the lemon juice and add the soda water. Spoon the mixture into jugs. Add ice cubes and mint to decorate. Slices of lemon or orange also make an attractive addition.

Mint tea makes a refreshing summer drink.

DECORATIVE ICE CUBES
Ice cubes containing herb flowers or leaves look especially pretty in summer drinks.
Half-fill the ice trays with water, and to each compartment add a flower, leaf
or sprig of herbs such as borage, mint, thyme, violets or lavender.
Top up with water and freeze in the usual way.

Festive Summertime Drinks

Here are two festive drinks that encapsulate the spirit of those lazy days of high summer. Serve them as delicious aperitifs to meals eaten al fresco, whether these be buffet parties in the garden, or leisurely Sunday lunches on the patio with friends.

MINT JULEP

This is the classic American drink that recalls the lifestyle of the Deep South. Made by the gallon on the first Saturday of May for the running of the famous Kentucky Derby, it has a history dating back to at least the early nineteenth century. The goal is to achieve a perfect balance between the flavours of bourbon – which gives the drink its kick – mint and sugar, with none of these dominating the others.

INGREDIENTS (FOR ONE)
1 teaspoon sugar
1 teaspoon water
5-6 large fresh mint leaves
Crushed ice
50ml/2fl. oz good-quality Kentucky bourbon
sprig of fresh mint, to decorate

Place the sugar, water and mint in the bottom of a tumbler. Mash with a spoon until the sugar is dissolved and the essence of the mint is extracted. Fill the glass with ice. When frost forms on the outside, slowly pour in the bourbon, allowing it to trickle through the ice, then stir. Decorate with the sprig of mint and serve immediately.

ELDERFLOWER CHAMPAGNE

This, of course, is not really a champagne, nor is it alcoholic, but it is a refreshing and deliciously fragrant drink to serve on a summer's day. Elder bushes grow wild in many places, so if you do not have one in your garden, take care where you pick the flowers. Avoid picking those that have been growing by the roadside, and always wash them before use.

*Selection of herb
and fruit wines.*

INGREDIENTS
4 litres/1 gal water
625g/1¼ lb caster sugar
2 juicy lemons
4 large elderflower heads
2 tablespoons white wine vinegar

Boil the water, then stir in the sugar until it has dissolved, and leave to cool. Squeeze out the juice from one lemon. Scrub the other lemon if it has been waxed, and cut into 4 pieces. Place the elderflowers in a large, non-metallic container. Add the lemon juice, lemon segments, the sweetened water and the vinegar. Stir, cover with a cloth, and leave for 24 hours. Strain the liquid through a fine sieve, squeezing the flowers to extract all the flavour. Pour into clean screw-top bottles, and leave for up to 10 days, until effervescent. Drink within 3-4 weeks.

Mint

HERBS FOR HEALTH

Herbs have been used in medicine throughout the world for centuries. Many people today are choosing to use herbal remedies as an alternative, or a complement, to modern medical treatments. Here we look at a few of the most common uses of herbs, to treat simple complaints and ailments.

Contents

Herbs for Health

INTRODUCTION

Before the invention of modern medicinal drugs, herbs were the chief form of medical remedy. The use of herbs for medicinal purposes dates back thousands of years. According to scientific research, medicinal herbs have been in use since about 3000 BC in China, and medicinal herbs are also believed to have been in use in ancient Egypt at around the same time.

In mediaeval Europe, great 'physick' gardens were established for the growing of culinary and medicinal herbs. Later, after the invention of printing, specialist books known as 'herbals' were published, which listed a vast number of herbs and their uses. One of the most famous was Nicholas Culpeper's The Complete Herbal, published in 1653.

With the rise of modern medicine and the development of surgical treatment, herbalism fell from favour. However, the growing concern about the known, and unknown, side-effects of medicinal drugs has led peopleto search for more natural and time-honoured forms of treatment, and herbalism is once more gaining popularity.

THE EFFECTIVENESS OF HERBS

The range of medicinal herbs is huge, and includes plants that many people would not think of as herbs at all. Wild flowers such as marsh mallow, cottage garden flowers such as calendula (pot marigold) and yarrow, flowering shrubs such as elderflower, even nettle and dandelion are just some of the many plants used in herbal medicine. The soft leaves and flowers, the woody bark and stems, and the tough seeds can all have medicinalproperties, depending on the plant involved.

Anyone who doubts the healing power of herbs should remember that the active ingredients in plants such as these have formed the basis for various modern drugs. Steroids and amphetamines have herbal origins, for example, and dixogin and digitoxin, used to treat the heart, are versions of digitalis, the active ingredient of foxgloves. Perhaps the most famous of all herbal derived medicines, though, is ordinary aspirin, which is based on willow bark, one of the best-known anti-inflammatory herbal remedies.

Aloe vera, a herbal remedy derived from a succulent of the aloe family, is another example of an ancient medicine providing effective treatment for modern illness.

Garlic has many medicinal uses.

Inhalations help sooth nasal congestion.

Research in the United States has shown aloe vera – whose use goes back to the fourth century BC – to be the best remedy for radiation burns.

Using Herbal Remedies

Herbs for medicinal use are available from specialist suppliers, but if you want to use fresh herbs, the safest option is grow your own, preferably organically.

Apart from herbal tablets which you can buy in health stores, making an infusion or decoction is the easiest way to take herbal remedies at home. These are best taken fresh while still hot, but they can be stored in the refrigerator for up to day. To make them more palatable, they may be sweetened with honey or apple juice.

MAKING AN INFUSION

Infusions are made by steeping the leaves, flowers, and soft stems of a herb in water. The quantities used depend on taste, and may be varied slightly to suit. Use 1–2 teaspoons of the dried herb, or double this quantity of the fresh herb. Place in a cup or teapot and pour over 1 cup of very hot, boiled water (the water should not be boiling as this would destroy too many of the herb's active constituents). Leave to stand for 10–20 minutes. Strain before drinking. For a larger quantity, enough for 3 daily doses, use up to 25 g/1 oz dried herb, or 50 g/2 oz fresh, to at least 600ml/1 pint of water.

MAKING A DECOCTION

Decoctions are made from the roots, bark, and sometimes the twigs, berries, or seeds of a plant. Because these are tougher, they need to be simmered in order to extract their active ingredients. To make a decoction, place 25 g /1 oz of a dried herb, or 50 g/2 oz

A marigold lotion eases scratches and abrasions.

fresh, broken or cut into pieces, into an enamelled, glass, or stainless steel saucepan (do not use aluminium). Cover with 900 ml /1^{1}/$_{2}$ pints water, bring to the boil, reduce the heat and simmer for 10–15 minutes until the liquid is reduced by two-thirds. Strain, sweeten if liked, and drink.

THINKING ABOUT SAFETY

Although herbal remedies, used correctly, have a good safety record, you should start with a lower than usual strength of a particular remedy to test for any adverse reaction. Herbs work best on an empty stomach, but if this makes you feel nauseous, take the herb either with, or just after, a meal. For adults, the usual dosage is one cup three times a day. Children below the age of five should not be given more than a quarter of the adult dose. From five to eleven years, they may take half the adult dose. People over 65 should also be particularly cautious,

A comfrey poultice relieves the discomfort of skin complaints.

as should anyone who suffers from allergies. Pregnant or breastfeeding women, or anyone taking prescribed drugs, should consult their doctor before taking any herbal remedy.

If you feel nauseous or have headaches or diarrhoea within two hours of taking a remedy, stop immediately, and consult your doctor or qualified herbalist. And remember – if a condition persists for more than a couple of days, you should always seek professional advice.

Relieving Aches and Pains

If you suffer from tension headaches or migraines, there are several herbal remedies to help you, two of which are listed below. Since stress and anxiety can contribute to these conditions, try to find ways of relaxing, too.

LAVENDER OIL

This oil, which is not the essential oil of aromatherapy (see pages 110–11), may be used to treat tension headache and migraines.

INGREDIENTS
handful of fresh flowers
1 litre/35fl. oz olive oil

Place the flowers and the oil in a glass jar or bottle, and leave to steep for 3 days in a sunny place. Strain through a fine filter, pressing the flowers as you do so. Repeat the process with a fresh handful of flowers, until the oil is highly perfumed. Take 5–6 drops per day on a lump of sugar.

VARIATIONS
Use the oil to massage the shoulders and neck where muscular tension builds leading to tension headaches. Dab the oil on the temples, too. Alternatively make a standard infusion of leaves and flowers (see page 101), and take 3 times daily.

CLARY SAGE

The volatile oil of clary sage (*Salvia sclarea*) – a member of the sage family – can be used as a gentle rub to relieve menstrual cramps. The

oil is of the kind used in aromatherapy (see pages 110–11), and should not be applied directly to the skin but should be diluted in a base oil.

INGREDIENTS
3 drops clary sage essential oil
1 teaspoon (5ml) almond oil

Combine 30 drops of clary sage oil with 50ml/2fl. oz base oil (or halve the quantities if preferred). Use to massage the lower abdomen and small of the back.

Lavender forms the basis of many soothing remedies.

FEVERFEW

Feverfew (*Chrysanthemum parthenium*) has been proved to be effective against migraine. It contains a volatile oil and tannin, and works by opening up the constricted blood vessels that cause the headache. It also has anti-arthritic properties. Use the leaves to make an infusion (see page 101), and take a small cup 3 times daily.
Caution: Some people recommend eating the leaves raw in salads. However, these can have an irritant effect and may cause mouth ulcers, so it is best to avoid using them in this way. Also avoid taking feverfew during pregnancy.

HERBS FOR RELAXATION

Try these remedies to help you relax and give you a good night's sleep: chamomile infusion (made to standard recipe, see page 101) valerian, taken as 25 drops of liquid tincture at bedtime lavender oil – a few drops on either side of your pillow to inhale

Feverfew

Relieving Cuts, Stings and Skin Problems

Flowers and leaves form the basis of these herbal remedies for the relief and treatment of various skin problems and minor wounds. Several are fragrant, too, and so offer a treat for the senses at the same time as healing the body.

CHAMOMILE OIL

A comfrey poultice relieves the discomfort of skin complaints.

A fragrant oil made from the flowers of chamomile (Chamaemelum nobilis) can be used to relieve allergic skin rashes.

INGREDIENTS
chamomile flower heads
olive oil

Tightly pack a jar with chamomile flowers, and cover with olive oil. Leave to infuse in a sunny place for 3 weeks, then strain, bottle and seal.

SALAD BURNET COMPRESS

To soothe sunburn, try making a compress with the leaves of salad burnet (*Sanguisorba minor*).

INGREDIENTS
handful of salad burnet leaves
600ml/1 pint hot, boiled water
gauze dressing

Lightly bruise the leaves, place in a bowl and pour over the hot water. Leave to steep for 10 minutes, then strain and allow to cool. Soak the dressing in the infusion and apply to the sunburnt area as often as necessary, until the treatment brings relief.

CAUTION
Do not take comfrey internally. Do not use for mastitis as it may be ingested by the baby during breastfeeding.

MARIGOLD LOTION

This lotion made from the flowers of that cottage-garden favourite, pot marigold

COMFREY

Another name for comfrey (*Symphytum officinale*) is 'knitbone' because it was traditionally used in the healing of bones - a poultice made from the root dries to a very hard consistency and, before the availability of plaster casts, provided a useful support. Comfrey is indeed one of the best-known and most useful medicinal herbs, having the ability to speed the healing of wounds. Make a poultice, as for salad burnet, and use to:
heal severe cuts, sprains, eczema, skin ulcers, haemorrhoids, psoriasis
soothe pain and inflammation
drain boils and abscesses.

INSTANT POULTICE

Yarrow leaves (*Achillea millefolium*) can be used as an instant poultice for minor cuts and wounds. Place the leaves briefly in boiling water, remove, allow to cool, then apply to the affected part.

LAVENDER OIL

Dab neat lavender oil onto an insect bite for instant relief from itching, redness and swelling.

(Calendula officinalis), provides useful relief for scratches and abrasions.

INGREDIENTS
75g/3oz dried marigold flowers
900ml/1½ pints hot, boiled water
aqueous cream, available from pharmacists

Infuse the flowers in the water for about 1 hour, then strain through muslin, squeezing out as much of the liquid as possible. Mix one part of the infusion with four parts of the cream, pour into a jar or bottle, seal, and store in the refrigerator until needed.

A marigold lotion eases scratches and abrasions.

Relieving Digestive Problems

There are various herbal remedies to help relieve digestive and urinary problems and, as so often happens, they bring other benefits, too. Ginger, for example, helps to relieve menstrual pains as well as nausea, while parsley both soothes the cramps of menstruation and is an effective diuretic.

GINGER INFUSION

You may not have ginger (*Zingiberis officinalis*) growing in your garden, but both the fresh root and its dried, powdered form are available in grocery stores and supermarkets. It contains volatile oils and phenols and is effective in relieving nausea, morning sickness and travel sickness. It can be irritating to the stomach so it is best to take it in small doses, especially during pregnancy.

Ginger is an effective relief from digestive complaints

INGREDIENTS
about 50g/2oz fresh ginger root
900ml/1½ pints water
honey to sweeten, if required

Slice the root and place in an enamelled or stainless steel saucepan with the water. Bring to simmering point and simmer for 10–15 minutes, until the liquid has reduced to about 600ml/1 pint. Allow to cool, sweeten with honey if preferred, and dilute to taste if necessary. Sip in small quantities as required.

VARIATIONS
Good-quality, powdered ginger of a sufficient quantity to suit individual taste may be used instead of the fresh root. As well as relieving nausea, ginger decoction is also beneficial for:
menstrual cramps
flatulence
problems associated with poor circulation, such as chilblains
cold and flu symptoms

MEADOWSWEET INFUSION

Meadowsweet (*Filipendula ulmaria*) is a natural source of salicylic acid, which is the active ingredient in aspirin. However, unlike aspirin, it does not irritate the stomach because its other constituents have a beneficial effect on the digestive system. It is astringent, anti-acidic and anti-inflammatory, and is useful in cases of excess acidity, indigestion, and diarrhoea.

DANDELION

Dandelion, that common garden weed, is in fact a useful diuretic. Take an infusion (see page 101) 3 times daily for the fluid retention that occurs pre-menstrually, or is due to a urinary infection or heart problem. Diuretic drugs used in treatment of the latter remove potassium from the body, a mineral vital to the effective functioning of the heart. The natural potassium content of dandelions helps to replace this loss, giving the plant a dual benefit.

BERGAMOT INFUSION

An infusion of bergamot, made in the usual way (see page 101), is soothing and relaxing and relieves nauseasymptoms and vomiting.

CRYSTALLIZED GINGER

To combat travel sickness, nibble a small pieces of crystallized ginger both before and during, your journey.

PARSLEY

Parsley is a natural diuretic, and is also an effective breath freshener, so chew some fresh parsley for sweet breath after a strongly flavoured meal. (But avoid during pregnancy).

A ginger infusion eases stomach discomfort and nausea.

INGREDIENTS

25g/1oz meadowsweet flowers
600ml/1 pint water boiling water
honey to sweeten (optional)

Place the flowers and water in a glass, enamelled or earthenware container, and leave to infuse for 10 minutes. Strain the liquid, dilute to taste if necessary, and sweeten with honey if liked. Take as 3 doses during the day.

VARIATIONS

Meadowsweet infusion may also be used to relieve the symptoms of:
arthritis and rheumatism

Introduction to Aromatheraphy

Aromatherapy is a form of healing massage which uses essential oils extracted from certain plants. It was invented by a French chemist, René-Maurice Gattefosse, after he had accidentally discovered that lavender oil had the ability to heal burns. Lavender oil is a perfect example of the efficacy of essential oils, for not only can it heal burns and relieve insect bites, but it is also a known antidote to the venom of the lethal black widow spider. Here are some ways you can enjoy the benefits of aromatherapy at home.

LOCAL MASSAGE

If you want to massage a specific area, say, the neck and shoulders, you should not, with a few exceptions, apply neat oil directly to the skin. Instead, mix up to 30 drops of essential oil to 50ml/2fl. oz base oil (almond, jojoba, avocado or other oils, available from health stores and pharmacies).

ADDING OILS TO THE BATH

Run a very warm bath, and add 6–8 drops of a single oil, or mixture of oils. Swirl the water so that the oil forms a scented film over the surface – do not add to running water or it will evaporate. Soak in the bath for 10–15 minutes.

INHALATION

Pour half a cup of hot water into a bowl and add 10 drops of oil. Lean over the bowl, cover your head with a towel and inhale the steam until the scent has almost evaporated. Repeat 3 times a day, but avoid if you suffer from asthma. Alternatively, place 10 drops of oil on a handkerchief or tissue, hold it to your nose, and breathe in. To relieve a blocked nose while you sleep, place the handkerchief or tissue on your pillow.

COMMON ESSENTIAL OILS

Here are some of the better-known essential oils, and the conditions they can treat:

Basil – Depression, stress, digestive problems
Bergamot – Cold sores, ulcers, sore throat
Cedarwood – Coughs, bronchitis, anxiety
Chamomile – Skin problems, nervous tension, neuralgia, digestive problems, insomnia, rheumatism
Cinnamon – Fatigue, infections, impotence, snakebites
Clary sage – Menstrual problems, high blood pressure
Clove – Infections, nervous and muscular tension, fatigue
Cypress – Coughs, flu, wounds, nervous and muscular tension, diarrhoea, varicose veins, menopausal symptoms
Eucalyptus – Colds, flu, asthma, laryngitis, cuts, insect-repelling
Geranium – Neuralgia, poor circulation, urinary disorders, viral infections, wounds, burns, insect-repelling
Juniper – Fatigue, insomnia, water retention, rheumatism
Lavender – Depression, headaches, digestive problems, wounds, burns, acne, insect and snake bites, insect-repelling
Lemon – Poor circulation, stomach upsets, water retention, acne
Neroli – Depression, panic, stress, nervous

tension, insomnia

Patchouli – Depression, anxiety, skin problems, wounds

Peppermint – Fatigue, indigestion, flatulence, travel sickness, headaches, bronchitis, asthma

Pine – Flu, asthma, fatigue, water retention, cystitis

Rose – Depression, headaches, nausea, insomnia

Rosemary – Fatigue, colds, flu, bronchitis, poor memory, rheumatism, sores, burns

Sage – Poor circulation, bronchitis, asthma, water retention, fatigue, nervousness, rheumatism, menopausal problems

Tea tree – Colds, sore throat, thrush

Thyme – Fatigue, digestive problems, asthma, infections, rheumatism, skin inflammations, intestinal parasites, snakebites

Aromatherapy oils can be used to ease discomfort, or aid relaxation.

*Herbal preparations
are easy to make.*

alternative methods of testing. Sadly, some manufacturers still test their products on animals, in some instances because they are constrained by laws regarding public safety.

In making your own herbal beauty preparations, you can generally rest assured that no suffering has been involved in their production. There can be a problem, however, if you are using a commercial product, such as a ready-made shampoo, as

the basis for your own herbal preparation. If you want to be absolutely sure, there are small, specialized manufacturers who guarantee that their beauty products - which are every bit as good as those of the major producers – are cruelty-free. You can find their names and brochures in health stores and some pharmacies.

Finally, making your own beauty preparations is fun! You can, of course, if you wish, spend time searching out the most obscure ingredients and slaving over a hot stove as you concoct your latest brew, but none of this is necessary. The recipes that follow have been chosen for their simplicity. They mostly involve herbs that you can grow yourself and require no special skills or equipment to make. Even where a recipe calls for an ingredient that you are unlikely to have at hand, it should still be easy to buy at your local grocery store, supermarket or pharmacy. There is absolutely no point in trying to make herbal remedies that demand a lot of effort. In our busy modern lives, no one has that kind of time to spare and the end result would simply be a return to buying your beauty preparations off the shelf.

MAKING AND STORING

As with culinary and medicinal herbs, remember that the dried form is twice as powerful as its fresh counterpart. For convenience and practicality, dried herbs are best chopped rather than finely ground.

Another useful tip to remember is that if you are making a preparation with milk, such as a facial wash, you do not to heat the herb to extract its essence. Cold milk can do this without heat: allow 1 tablespoon of the dried herb to every 225ml/8fl. oz milk, cover and steep for a few hours.

Because homemade herbal preparations are completely natural and contain no preservatives, it is best to keep them in the refrigerator, especially those that contain fatty substances such as milk or buttermilk. On their own, infusion-based preparations such as hair rinses will last for about a week, but the addition of a little spirit, such as rum, will extend their keeping time. For the same reason, do not make herbal preparations in large quantities.

Herbal rinses revitalise your hair.

Cleansing the Skin

If you want your skin to look good, you must begin by cleansing it thoroughly to rid it of old make-up and – particularly if you live in a city – the dust and grime that it will inevitably collect in an urban environment. The skin acts as a filtering mechanism for the body and produces its own impurities, and these need removing, too. Here are some simple herbal cleansers that provide a delightful and easy-to-make alternative to commercial preparations.

COMFREY CLEANSING OIL

Steam opens the pores to cleanse the skin.

This is a gentle cleansing oil that is especially suitable for dry skin. Apply to the face with cotton wool pads.

INGREDIENTS
comfrey leaves (see method)
300ml/¹/2 pint almond oil

Fill a jar with the oil, and add as many comfrey leaves as the oil can cover. Seal the jar and leave the leaves to steep in a warm place for 2–3 weeks. Shake the jar regularly. Strain the oil, bottle, seal, and use as required.

ELDERFLOWER CLEANSING CREAM

Generations of women have relied on preparations made from elderflowers to keep their skin fair and free of blemishes. Here is an almost edible cream made from this herb that may be used to cleanse the skin.

INGREDIENTS
5 tablespoons of fresh elderflowers
300ml/¹/2 pint buttermilk
2 tablespoons honey

Gently heat the buttermilk and immerse the elderflowers in it. Continue to simmer for about ½ hour until the blossoms soften. Remove from the heat and leave to infuse for a further 3 hours. Reheat, then strain and add the honey. Bottle, seal, and store in the refrigerator.

for general use: chamomile, elderflower
to cleanse and soothe: chamomile (with thyme and lavender, if liked), lady's mantle
to remove impurities: fennel, nettle
to correct oiliness: yarrow
to cleanse and boost circulation: nettle, rosemary
to stimulate and tighten: peppermint, elderflower
to heal: comfrey, fennel

ROSEMARY CLEANSING LOTION

Here is a quick way to adapt a ready-made cleansing cream for use on oily skin. Add 1 tablespoon of a strong rosemary infusion (see page 101) to 125g/4oz good-quality, non-scented cleansing cream, stirring well to combine.

STEAM TREATMENT

Herbs may be added to a facial steam bath to cleanse and improve the skin in various ways. Pour boiling water over a handful of your chosen herb, place a towel over your head to make a 'steam tent', and allow the vapour to soak your face for 10 minutes or more. Close your pores by splashing with cool water, or using a toner (see pages 120–1), and avoid going out for at least an hour afterwards.

Herbal treatments are kind to your skin.

Toners and Soothers

After cleansing, the next step in your beauty routine is to tone the skin in order to remove any excess oiliness, to firm the tissues and to restore the skin's natural balance. Certain parts of the face may also need special treatment, for example, the lips where the skin is fine and prone to chapping, or the cheeks where thread veins can appear. Note that if you have thread veins, you should never steam your face or use hot water on it.

LAVENDER TONER

This toner, made from lavender flowers and vinegar, is a very ancient preparation. It is important to use cider vinegar as this restores the skin's acid mantle. It also softens the skin and remedies any itchiness due to dryness. The mixture may be made in smaller quantities if liked.

INGREDIENTS
6 tablespoons lavender flowers
600 ml/1 pint cider vinegar
1200ml/2 pints water

Add the lavender flowers to the vinegar and leave to steep for two weeks. Strain, add the water, bottle and seal. Store in a cool, dark place.

YARROW AND CHAMOMILE ASTRINGENT

The properties of these two herbs make this an excellent astringent for oily skin.

INGREDIENTS
2 tablespoons fresh, or 1 tablespoon dried, yarrow flowers
2 tablespoons fresh, or 1 tablespoon dried, chamomile flowers
300 ml/¹/₂ pint boiling water

Pour the water over the flowers, stir, cover, and leave to steep in a warm place for 30 minutes. Strain, bottle andseal. Apply with cotton wool, after cleansing, or as required.

COLTSFOOT COMPRESS

To treat thread veins, pat the affected area with milk, leave for 15 minutes, then wash off with a soft cloth and tepid water. Then apply a coltsfoot compress made according to the instructions on page 101, or by steeping 1 tablespoon of the dried herb, or 2 tablespoons fresh, in 300ml/½ pint milk for a few hours, covered.

MARIGOLD LOTION

A lotion made from the leaves of pot marigold (Calendula officinalis) is a very old folk remedy for thread veins. Make a standard infusion (see page 101) and leave to steep for 20 minutes to 3 hours. Strain and pat on the affected area.

HONEY AND LAVENDER LIP BALM

Combine a few drops of lavender infusion (see page 101) with 2 tablespoons of clarified honey. Store in a sealed, labelled jar, and rub on your lips at bedtime to heal chapped skin.

Lavender toner is one of the oldest herbal beauty treatments.

Hair Care

Herbal infusions can do much to enhance your natural hair colour, to improve the condition of your hair. Add them to shampoos or the final rinse water, or use them in a nightly massage routine to banish greyness or eliminate dandruff.

MULLEIN AND CHAMOMILE HAIR RINSE

Chamomile is a well-known natural lightener for fair hair. The addition of mullein to this mixture will give the hair a golden glow.

INGREDIENTS
25g/1oz dried or 50g/2 oz fresh chamomile flowers
25g/1oz dried or 50g/2 oz fresh mullein flowers
2 tablespoons lemon juice
600ml/1 pint water

Bring the water to the boil, then pour over the flowers. Leave to infuse for 30-60 minutes, strain, add the lemon juice, and use as a final rinse after shampooing.

Sage

VARIATIONS

If you simply want to lighten the hair, make a chamomile rinse with a handful of flowers to 600ml/1 pint water, and leave to steep for 20 minutes to 3 hours. Alternatively, a simple rinse made with mullein leaves will give the hair a golden tinge.

NETTLE DANDRUFF TONIC

Nettle juice is a traditional herbal hair remedy, and is considered especially effective in treating dandruff.

INGREDIENTS
4 tablespoons nettle leaves
600ml/1 pint boiling water
50ml/2fl. oz cider vinegar
50ml/2fl. oz eau de cologne

Pour the water over the nettle leaves, cover, and leave to steep for several hours. Strain, add the vinegar and eau de cologne, bottle and seal. If your hair is very greasy, double the quantity of eau de cologne. Massage into the scalp nightly.

SAGE TEA FOR GREY HAIR

If you have naturally dark hair that is turning grey, try this traditional remedy. Rub the preparation into the scalp four or five times a week. The greyness will gradually disappear and your hair will be returned to its original dark hue.

INGREDIENTS
1 tablespoon dried sage
1 tablespoon tea
600ml/1 pint boiling water
1 tablespoon rum, gin or eau-de-Cologne

ROSEMARY RINSE

Rosemary is a traditional 'pick-me-up'
for dark hair, helping to restore its colour
and adding lustre. It is also said
to be useful in the treatment of dandruff.
Simply make an infusion (see page 101)
and add to the final rinse water.

CATMINT HAIR TONIC

An infusion of catmint, added to the
final rinse water after shampooing, is a
traditional gypsy remedy to increase
hair growth and help prevent baldness.

*Herbs such as
chamomile and
mullein enhance
the colour and
shine of your hair.*

Place the sage and tea in a large jar, pour
over the water and seal. Place the jar in a
saucepan half-filled with water, and simmer
for 2 hours, topping up the water in the
saucepan as necessary. Allow to cool and
strain, then add the rum, gin or
eau-de-Cologne, if using. If not, the mixture
will keep for about one week.

Bath Time

Most beauty routines concentrate on the face, often neglecting the rest of the body. But the skin on the legs, arms, hands and elsewhere needs care, too, and amply repays any extra attention given to it. For easy, all-over skin care with the minimum of effort, turn bathtime into a beauty routine with these herbal preparations.

Herbal bath recipes

Adding certain herbs to the bath can make bathtime more than just a pleasant way to relax and cleanse the skin. To prevent the herbs clinging to your skin when you emerge, suspend them in a muslin bag from the tap so that the water runs through them, or use an individual stainless steel tea infuser in the same way. Fresh or dried herbs may be used, but the dried variety will have a more powerful aroma.

chamomile (fresh leaves and flowers, or dried flowers): soothes the skin
chamomile (as above), with a little rosemary, **horsetail and pine needles** (or extract): stimulates the skin
elder leaves, flowers, berries and bark: lightens, heals and stimulates the skin
lady's mantle (whole plant): heals inflamed skin
pot marigold (*Calendula officinalis*) **leaves:** heals scars and thread veins, soothes varicose veins
yarrow (leaves and flowers): reduces skin oiliness
nettle and dandelion (leaves): cleanses the skin, balances hormones
mint (whole plant): heals minor skin eruptions

Bath oil

Homemade herbal bath oils are far purer than the commercially prepared varieties, and have a more authentic fragrance. The almond or almond-avocado oil used in this recipe will float on the water and cling to your skin as you emerge from the bath.

Ingredients
125ml/4fl. oz almond oil, or 75ml/3fl. almond oil and 25ml/1fl. oz avocado oil
10–15 drops essential oil (see pages 110–11)

Combine the oils, bottle, seal and label. Store in a cool, dark place. Use one teaspoon per bath.

Herbal milk bath

Milk baths are a beauty treatment which Cleopatra is said to have indulged in. However, you don't need to imitate Cleopatra who probably filled an entire tub with milk; all you need to do is add about 600ml/1 pint – or more, if possible – to a warm bath for an extra special, all-over treatment. Milk is both nourishing and soothing and will soften your entire skin as well as giving it a lustrous finish. For an additional softening effect, add a strong infusion of elderflower, chamomile or nettle (see page 101) to the bath water along with the milk.

VINEGAR BATHS

The effectiveness of herb baths can be increased by including cider vinegar in the bath routine. Simply add 225ml/8fl. oz cider vinegar to the bathwater to relieve the itchiness and flakiness of dry skin. Or, to relieve fatigue, massage the neck, shoulders, back and arms with cider vinegar before slipping into your herb-scented bath.

Home-made herbal bath oils and milks are purer, and fresher-smelling than commercial brands.

Soaps and Flower Waters

Herbs can be added to various household preparations to bring a fresh, country fragrance to your home. It is the small touches such as a homemade soap or herb-scented linen that will make your home an even more pleasant place to be.

LAVENDER SOAP

This recipe makes a liquid soap with a delightful lavender scent. Keep it in an attractive bottle by the side of the bath or handbasin.

INGREDIENTS
10 tablespoons finely grated Castile soap (available from good pharmacists), or pure soap flakes
8 tablespoons boiling water
2 tablespoons dried lavender flowers, crushed to a powder
4 drops of essential oil of lavender

Combine the soap and water in a heat proof bowl. Place over a saucepan of simmering water, and stir until the soap melts to a smooth consistency. Remove from the heat and add the lavender flowers and lavender oil. Pour into a bottle, seal and label.

EASY LAVENDER WATER

Although this does not have the keeping qualities of distilled flower waters, here is an almost instant lavender water which is simplicity itself to make. It can, of course, be used as a splash after the bath, and an attractive bottle placed on a bedside table

would make a pleasant welcome for a guest. Or you could revive the delightful, old-fashioned custom of finger bowls – small bowls of refreshing water containing a dash of this fragrant lavender mixture in which diners can dip their fingers at the end of a meal – especially useful after eating 'finger foods' such as cheese and biscuits or fruit.

INGREDIENTS
600ml/1 pint water
3 drops essential oil of lavender
1 lump of sugar

Combine the ingredients in a sealed container and shake until they are well mixed and the sugar has dissolved.

VARIATIONS
Try other essential oils instead of lavender. Lemony or sweet perfumes would work best.

HERBAL RINSING WATER

To scent household linen, add this costmary infusion to the final rinsing water. Nowadays, most people wash large items such as sheets in a washing machine, so this method is probably only practicable for smaller items such as tea towels, pillow cases or napkins, or any other delicate items that you do not want to subject to a machine wash. You could also try using it if hand-washing underwear. Costmary will also repel insects.

INGREDIENTS

*50g/2oz dried or 125g/4oz fresh costmary
leaves
600ml/1 pint boiling water*

Place the costmary in a bowl and pour over
the water. Cover and leave to steep for a
minimum of 2 hours. Strain and use as
described above.

*Herbal soaps are
refreshing, and
make creative gift
ideas.*

Herbs around the Home

The most familiar domestic use for herbs is, of course, the potpourri, made from dried, or semi-dried, leaves, petals and flowerbuds. Ready-made potpourris in various combinations of plant material are now widely available in gift shops and florists. Buying a potpourri mixture is the easy option, but making your own at home has the advantage that you can choose the exact ingredients to suit your personal preference. How much nicer it is, too, to perfume a room with natural aromas than the artificial perfume of a modern air freshener from a spray can.

DECORATIVE USES

Dried herbs and flowers can also be used to decorate the home when fresh flowers are scarce. Stuffed into baskets, gathered together to make 'tussie-mussies' – tiny bunches of fragrant flowers and herbs - or arranged in seasonal wreaths, they can adorn tables and walls. These dried arrangements will also last much longer than fresh ones.

PRACTICAL PURPOSES

Although we now think of herbs in the home as a purely sensual treat, pleasing either the nose or the eye, in the past herbs were used domestically for much more practical, down-to-earth purposes. As with medicines and cosmetics, the manufacture of domestic products to cleanse and freshen the home and keep it germ- and pest-free has become a huge, commercial industry. However, this was not always so. The herb garden, hedgerow or field that once provided the raw ingredients for the medicinal and

Herbs have many decorative uses at home.

cosmetic preparations on which people depended also provided them with a way of keeping their homes sweet-smelling (in the days before modern sanitation) and hygienic.

One common practice was to strew certain herbs, for example, lavender, catmint or tansy, in places where a pest infestation might occur. Depending on the herb used, this could help to deter such unwanted visitors as fleas or rats. Another practice – that of placing herb-filled sachets in wardrobes or drawers – was done not just to perfume their contents but to keep pests at bay. In Elizabethan times, for example, lavender bags were placed among household linens and blankets to deter moths. Other herbs valued for their insect-repelling properties were pennyroyal, a species of mint, for fleas; rue, for fleas and other insects; southernwood, for various insects including moths; and tansy, for flies.

Herbs were employed against illness, too. Lavender stems were burnt as a fumigant in the sickroom, and rue was also burnt as an air cleanser. The tussie-mussies mentioned above were originally used in medieval times to ward off the infection and unpleasant smells from plague and other diseases.

Herbs can be dried or frozen.

REST AND RELAXATION

THE NATURAL WAY

A pleasant way to combine both the sensual and practical uses of herbs in the home is to make a herb cushion or pillow, filled with a dried mixture, to use as an aid to sleep. The weight and warmth of your head will release the fragrance of the herbs, and feelings of stress and tension will float away. A few drops of an essential oil in an oil burner can have a similar effect. The oil is placed in a little water in the upper container of the burner; the heat from a burning night light in the lower compartment warms the water and the fragrance of the oil wafts out on the water vapour. Oil burners should, however, never be left unattended for any length of time – and should certainly not be used when you are going to sleep at night – because the water can evaporate surprisingly quickly leaving the candle burning on.

The trend towards more traditional and natural ways of doing things that are healthy and do not harm the environment or other living creatures – in the foods we eat, the medicines we take, the cosmetics we use – seems to lead inevitably to the use of herbal products in the home. The more this awareness of health and environmental issues grows, the more people will become concerned about the harmful effects of such products as, say, domestic flea or fly sprays, and the more they will look for safer alternatives: this is where herbs can be helpful, just as they were for our ancestors over the centuries, in so many areas of their lives.

Mixing your selection of flowers and petals

Potpourris

Potpourris are aromatic mixtures of flower petals, leaves and other ingredients that can bring the scents of summer to your home all year round. Remember that your potpourri is going to be on show, so choose plant material for its appearance as well as its scent – prettily shaped buds and leaves will add aesthetic appeal to the mixture. The method described below is for a dry potpourri which is easier and quicker to make than the moist type.

MAKING A POTPOURRI

Gather and dry your ingredients in the same way as you would culinary and medicinal herbs (see pages 145–9), separating out the petals of larger flowers and keeping smaller buds whole. Drying the flowers in dark conditions is especially important if you want to preserve their colour. When the flowers and leaves are crisp, but not powdery, they are ready for use. Only observation will tell when they reach this stage – it can vary from a day to a week or longer. The proportions below are for a fairly standard mix, which you may like to vary slightly as your experience grows.

INGREDIENTS
450g/1 lb whole buds, petals and leaves
1 tablespoon ground spices
1 tablespoon orris root powder
3 drops essential oil

The orris root, available from some health stores, pharmacists and florists, acts as a fixative which, along with the oil, brings the different aromas together and stabilizes the scent of the potpourri. Mix together the flowers, leaves and spices in a large, airtight jar (ideally earthenware, and not metal). Keep covered and stir daily for 4 days. Then add the orris root and essential oil, cover and leave for another 6 weeks, stirring daily if possible.

SUGGESTED POTPOURRI MIXES

Selecting ingredients for a potpourri is very much a personal choice, also dependent on what you have available. Here are some combinations to start you off.

ROSE POTPOURRI

rose petals
scented geranium leaves and petals
small quantity rosemary and lavender
cinnamon and cloves
rose and lavender oils

LEMON AND SPICE POTPOURRI

rose petals
a mixture of equal parts marigold,
carnation and azalea petals
lemon verbena leaves
small quantity thyme
rose and carnation oils

MIXED HERB POTPOURRI

rose petals
lavender, rosemary, bay, southernwood
cloves and allspice
sandalwood oil

A beautiful rose
pot-pourri

Pillows and Pouches

Potpourri mixes can be used in a whole variety of sachets and cushions, designed for different purposes. When closing up the opening after filling, use loose stitches, or seal the opening with Velcro. That way, you can easily open the sachet or cushion at a later date when you want to refresh or replace the filling.

PLACE MAT

Make a place mat from a piece of quilted cotton wadding and a piece of pretty cotton fabric. Fill with the potpourri mix of your choice (see pages 134–5). When a hot dish or teapot is placed on the mat, the heat will release its fragrance.

SCENTED PADS

This clever, old-fashioned recipe produces not one finished item, but two – an aromatic oil for toiletry use, and scented pads to perfume drawers and cupboards.

INGREDIENTS
Olive oil
Fresh aromatic flowers and leaves of your choice
Cotton wool or wadding

Steep the cotton wool or wadding in the olive oil until it is thoroughly soaked and heavy with oil. Place a layer in an earthenware jar. Cover with a layer of flowers and leaves. Repeat the layering of cotton wool and plant material until the jar is full. Seal and stand in a sunny place for 1 week. Remove the flowers and leaves and press the oil, now impregnated with the plant aromas, from the cotton wool or wadding. Pour into a bottle and seal. Use the cotton wool to perfume drawers and chests.

SWEET BAGS

These bags use a mixture of dried aromatic leaves and flowers. They may be placed in drawers and cupboards to scent them, beneath pillows where they will release their perfume when you lay your head down or – and perhaps most pleasing of all – hung over the backs of chairs where they will again give off their scent under the warmth and pressure of the body. Make the bags from muslin or a lightweight fabric in whatever shape you choose, leaving an opening for the filling. Add loops to hang the bags by, if wished.

Fill with a pot pourri mixture of your choice (see pages 134–5), then stitch up the opening or close with Velcro.

VARIATIONS

Lavender bags are made the same way, using the dried flower heads as filling.

SLEEP PILLOWS

Make a small cushion and fill with a potpourri mix containing dried lavender and chamomile flowers, and dried hops, and use it to soothe you to sleep.

Wreaths and Table Decorations

Although most dried arrangements use flowers, herbs – some of which have attractive flower- or seed-heads of their own – can make decorative arrangements, too, and they have the added benefit of being aromatic.

POTPOURRI AND POSY RING

This decorative wreath takes the colour, texture and aroma of a floral potpourri mixture and transforms them into an irrestibly pretty decoration.

MATERIALS
15cm/6in straw wreath form
Potpourri (see pages 134-5)
1m/1yd velvet ribbon, 2.5cm/1in wide
Selection of dried flowers
Medium-gauge florist's wire
Fine-gauge floral wire
Glue sticks and glue gun

If you are going to hang the wreath, begin by winding some medium-gauge wire around it to make a discreet loop. Gather the dried flowers into a posy and cut the stems short, then bind them with a piece of fine-gauge floral wire. Spread a thick layer of glue on a small area of the wreath form (in front of the wire loop), then press some potpourri firmly onto the glue. Make some medium-gauge wire into a U-shaped staple, place the posy over the potpourri, and press it firmly onto the wreath form with the staple. Continue gluing potpourri to the form, working in small areas at a time, until the whole form is covered. Glue one end of the ribbon to the back of the form and gently wind it around the wreath. Attach the loose end with more glue.

HERB AND SPICE WREATH

Here is a decorative way of storing culinary herbs – make an aromatic wreath for your kitchen wall with dried bay leaves and other herbs. Any herbs that are glued to the wreath, rather than attached with wire, will not of course be edible.

MATERIALS
Selection of herbs and spices, such as bay leaves, fennel stems and seedheads, marjoram flowers, purple sage leaves, star anise, garlic corms, cinnamon sticks, dried red and green chillies
Raffia, for bow
25cm/10in wreath form
Medium-gauge florist's wire
Glue sticks and glue gun

Wind some wire around the wreath and form into a loop at the back by which to hang the wreath. Gather the herbs into bunches, trim the stems, and secure with wire, twisting the ends tightly at the back. Attach the bunches to the wreath form at intervals by pushing the wire through the back of the wreath and bending it flat. Attach the spices and the chillies in the same way, arranging them singly or in small clusters. Using the glue gun, glue the star anise (if using) to the wreath. Tie the raffia in a bow around the wreath.

LAVENDER BASKET

For a pretty bedside or table decoration, fill
a small basket with dried lavender. Twist a
length of purple or blue satin ribbon around
the handle, and finish in a bow.

A pretty posy

Gift Ideas

The suggestions here, as well as several of the recipes on the previous pages, would make attractive and unusual gifts – and all the more acceptable because the recipient knows that you have taken the trouble to make them yourself.

CATMINT MOUSE

Here is a toy to give to a feline friend. A clump of catmint is cat heaven, as any gardener will testify who has tried to grow the plant in open ground, only to have it flattened by a cat rolling over it in ecstasy. To make a catmint mouse, unpick a fabric toy mouse, remove the stuffing, replace with dried catmint leaves, and sew up the opening again. Alternatively make a muslin pouch and fill with the dried leaves.

DECORATIVE SCENTED CANDLE

Scented candles provide a special ambience in any room, each different scent providing a special mood. Cinnamon and cloves give a festive scent for Christmas, Frankincense and Patchouli create an Eastern mood, while Jasmine produces a fresh, spring-like fragrance. For more practical purposes, lemongrass can be used to eliminate old tobacco smells.

For a delicious cinnamon candle, you will need a plain orange or dark red coloured candle. This can be ready-scented, or if you choose, you can add the scent yourself. Do this by lighting the candle, and allowing some of the wax to melt. Then simply add a few drops of scented oil to the melted wax, extinguish the flame, and allow to cool. When next the candle is lit, the delicious aroma will be released.

To decorate, tie cinammon sticks around the candle with twine or scrim, fastening with pins. For added effect, add some cloves between each stick.

SCENTED NOTEPAPER

Turn ordinary notepaper into a special gift by scenting it with small sweetbags.

MATERIALS
Matching notepaper and envelopes
2-3 shallow sachets filled with potpourri mix (see Sweetbags, pages 136-7)
Attractive box to hold notepaper and envelopes, slightly deeper than the stationery
Cellophane, if box has no lid
Length of satin ribbon

Arrange the notepaper and envelopes in the box, slipping the sweetbags between the layers. Replace the lid or wrap with cellophane, and secure with the satin ribbon, finishing in a bow. The paper will soon absorb the scent of the potpourri, and the recipient can then use the sweetbags to perfume linen or lingerie.

Insect Repellents

While the distinctive aroma of herbs may please human nostrils, it has the power to repel unwanted domestic visitors, such as mosquitoes, fleas, moths and even rats. Using herbs is a more pleasant way to keep moths from stored garments and linens than the conventional moth balls, whose pungent smell seems to linger for ever.

COTTON LAVENDER MOTH REPELLENT

A mixture of cotton lavender and other herbs makes a useful moth repellent. Make sweet bags filled with the mixture and hang in wardrobes or place in cupboards or drawers to ward off moths, and to impart an aromatic scent to clothes and linen.

INGREDIENTS
Equal parts cotton lavender leaves, lavender flowers, rosemary leaves and rue, dried and crumbled

Combine the ingredients and use to fill bags made of lightweight fabric, adding ribbon loops for hanging if desired.

SOUTHERNWOOD MOTH REPELLENT

Southernwood is a well-known insect repellent. If you grow it, keep it well away from flowering plants as it will even repel bees. Used here with cinnamon, it provides another effective way to prevent moths invading woollen clothes stored away for the summer. Its role as a moth deterrent is enshrined in its French name – garderobe, literally 'clothes guard'.

INGREDIENTS
25g/1oz dried southernwood
1 teaspoon crushed cinnamon stick

Combine the ingredients and use to fill a small muslin bag. Add a ribbon loop to the bag and hang it over a coathanger, or just slip between stored garments.

CITRONELLA BURNER
Essential oil of citronella (Cymbopogon nardus) is distilled from a grass and used in aromatherapy. Try a few drops in an oil burner to keep away mosquitoes and other biting insects when you are sitting outdoors on warm summer nights. (To prevent the insects from biting you, rub your skin with lavender oil.)

STREWED CATMINT
A traditional rat repellent is to strew catmint leaves wherever the presence of the rodents is suspected. Bunches of catmint placed in hen and duck houses are said to deter rats there, too.

TANSY BUNCHES
A bunch of tansy leaves hanging in a room are a traditional fly repellent.

*Grind cinnamon
and southernwood
for an effective
moth repellent.*

Harvesting and Preserving Herbs

Fresh herbs can be cut for culinary, medicinal or cosmetic use throughout their growing season. However, if you want a year-round supply, you can dry or freeze herbs to preserve them for later use.

HARVESTING

The fragrance, flavour and value of a herb is contained in its volatile oils. If you want to achieve the best results from preserved herbs, you will therefore need to pick them when their volatile oil content is highest. There are two points to consider here: first, the time of day you gather the plants; and second, the plant's stage in its growing cycle.

When picking herbs for preserving, the best time is in the early morning after the dew has had a chance to dry naturally but before the sun is fully on the plant. In the full heat of the sun, the volatile plant oils diminish.

Choosing the right growing stage in a plant's cycle depends on the part of the plant you want to harvest. If you are going to preserve the leaves, the best time to gather them is after the flowerbuds have formed but before the flowers have opened. At this stage, the oil content of the leaves is highest. Flowers should be picked when they are fully open, and you should choose only those that are in prime condition. To gather the seeds, pick the flowerheads when they are turning brown. An easy way to check whether the seeds are ripe is to tap the flowerhead lightly;

if the seeds are ripe, they will fall readily.

DRYING HERBS

The traditional way to preserve herbs is to dry them. The aim in drying is to preserve as much of the herb's colour and scent as possible, so the faster they dry the better. However, this does not mean that you can speed the process up by placing them in the

Whole herbs can be dried by hanging.

Dried and ground herbs.

Herbs can be stored for use as a preserve or jelly at a later date.

oven – they must dry naturally. Dried herbs are ready when they feel brittle to the touch. Leaves and flowers should have retained their colour, however; if the leaves are brown and the flowers very faded, the heat used to dry them was too intense and the herbs will have lost their fragrance, flavour and value.

HANGING HERBS

This is the traditional method of drying herbs. All it involves is tying the plants, still on their stems, into small bunches and hanging them in a warm. well-ventilated spot where air can circulate freely through them, for a few days. Bunches of herbs

hanging from the ceiling or a rack is an almost essential design element of the country-style kitchen.

HERBS ON TRAYS

Another way to dry herbs is to spread them out on racks. Stretch or lay some muslin over some metal cake racks – the kind used to air cakes after baking. The muslin is necessary to stop smaller particles falling through the racks during drying. Arrange the leaves, still on their stems, over the muslin in a single layer. If you are drying flowerheads as well, remove as much stem from them as possible.

Place more muslin over the herbs to keep them free of dust, and leave in a warm, dark place to dry. An airing cupboard is ideal, but you could also use the plate-warming compartment of the cooker, with the door left open. The heat of the oven, when it is on, will be sufficient to warm the compartment and the open door will prevent over-heating. Check the herbs after 24 hours to see if they are dry.

MICROWAVING HERBS

Although herbs should not be dried in a conventional oven, the way in which microwave ovens disperse heat offers another, extremely fast of way of drying them. The method is, however, best suited to leaves only as flowerheads can lose their shape. It is also best to stick to one variety of herb at a time, as different herbs have different drying rates.

Spread a small quantity of your chosen herb on a double layer of kitchen towel, and place on the turntable of the oven. Cover with a second double layer of towel. Turn the oven to its lowest setting, set the timer to 60 seconds, and switch on. At the end of this time, check to see how the herb is progressing, and continue in intervals of 60 seconds until drying is complete. Delicate-leaved herbs such as basil should be dry in 3–6 minutes, but coarser herbs such as rosemary may take as long as 10 minutes.

Herbs can be dried or frozen.

DRYING SEEDHEADS

Because of their size, seeds need a slightly different method of drying from other parts of a plant. When the seedheads are ready (see above), cut them, along with a length of stem, tie in bunches of two or three, and hang them, head-down, in a dry, airy place. To catch the seeds as they fall, either encase the heads in paper bags, or hang them over a basket lined with kitchen towel or cloth.

STORING DRIED HERBS

Dried herbs, including seeds, should be stored in airtight glass jars, in a dark place. Label the jars with the name of the herb, and the storage date. If dried herbs have lost their scent and colour, or if they smell at all musty or have gone mouldy, throw them away.

FREEZING HERBS

Certain culinary herbs respond well to freezing – in fact, some, such as basil, parsley, chives, chervil, dill and tarragon, are better preserved this way than dried. Parsley and chives should be coarsely chopped and stored in small freezer bags or containers; alternatively, freeze them in a little water in ice-cube containers. Basil leaves are best left whole and stored in bags. Sprays of chervil, fennel, dill and tarragon may also be packed into bags. Use frozen herbs as soon as they have thawed as they deteriorate quickly.

Oils, vinegars and jellies make delicious herb preserves.

Fresh, dried or frozen, herbs can be used all year round.

The Language of Herbs

As well as their culinary, medicinal and cosmetic uses, herbs were traditionally believed to have other properties and purposes. Bay, for example, was the herb associated with honour, and was used to crown heroes in Greek and Roman times, while borage was thought to bring courage and happiness; other herbs were used as protection against witchcraft. The names of herbs can also be revealing since they are based on ancient associations with particular plants. Learning the history and 'language' of herbs is a fascinating study, and brings an extra dimension to the growing and using of herbs. Some of the herbs that follow are still familiar today; others are less common. All have, however, at some point in history, had their own powerful associations for the people that used them.

ANGELICA

One of the most ancient herbs, angelica may have been used in pagan festivals and as a protection against witchcraft. Its botanical name, *Angelica archangelica*, derives from its habit of flowering around 8 May in the Old Style calender (the calender was adjusted by Pope Gregory in 1582 and a new one instituted), which is the feast day of the Archangel Michael.

DANDELION

The name 'dandelion' derives from dent de lion, or lion's tooth, perhaps an allusion to the shape of the leaves. Because of its diuretic properties, the herb was also known as 'piss-a-beds', a quality still remembered in its French name *pissenlit*.

FEVERFEW

Although it was not traditionally used as a remedy for high temperatures, the name 'feverfew' is a corruption of 'febrifuge' from the Latin *febris*, or fever, and *fugo*, to put to flight – in other words, the herb that makes fevers flee.

BERGAMOT

This herb is of American origin and strongly
associated with the original inhabitants of
North America. The Oswego Indians, in
particular, used the leaves to make a
drink, and at the time of the Boston
Tea Party of 1773, a protest against
the tea tax imposed by England,
American colonists substituted
bergamot for Indian tea. The plant is
much loved by bees, hence its other
common name, 'bee-balm'.

TARRAGON

Tarragon, or *Artemisia dracunculus*, was
believed to have the ability to heal the
bites of snakes and serpents, and this
property is alluded to in its name. Its common name come from esdragon, a French
corruption of the *dracunculus* of its botanical name, which means 'little dragon'.

COSTMARY

In colonial times in North America, leaves
of costmary were used as bookmarks in
bibles, giving rise to the herb's other common name, 'bible leaf'.

Bergamot

CLARY

The name 'clary' derives from 'clear-eye'
because it was traditionally used as a
medicinal remedy for the eyes.

RUE

The name 'rue' derives from the Greek word
reuo, which means 'to set free'. The herb
acquired its name because it was believed to
be effective in relieving so many ailments. It
is said to represent repentance and regret.

ELDER

There are numerous magical beliefs and customs associated with the elder. It was strongly linked with witches but, conversely, planting an elder bush outside the back door of a house would keep witches away. Cutting it, on the other hand, would bring bad luck. It was believed that lightning would never strike an elder, and that Christ's cross was made from its wood. The flowers of the elder are said to represent compassion and sympathy.

LOVAGE

This herb was once thought to be an aphrodisiac and was an essential ingredient of love potions – hence its name.

MARIGOLD

In medieval times, the pot marigold was commonly called 'Golds' or 'ruddes'. Its modern common name, 'marigold' derives from the Anglo-Saxon *merso-meagalla*, or marsh marigold. Its botanical name, *Calendula*, comes from the Latin *calends*, the Roman name for the first day of each month (from which we also get the word 'calendar') because the marigold was thought capable of blooming throughout the year.

LAVENDER

Lavender is associated with silence and the acceptance and recognition of love.

PARSLEY

Parsley is the herb of celebrations and festivities.

MARJORAM

Marjoram is thought to represent happiness. All the marjorams, including the Italian oregano, are known botanically as *riganum*, a name linked with the Greek cross, or mountain, and *ganos*, or joy and beauty. In Greece, the herb was traditionally woven into the crowns worn by bridal couples.

BAY

Bay, or laurel, is traditionally associated with honour and loyalty, as suggested by its botanical name, *Laurus nobilis* (noble laurel). The plant was dedicated to the Greek god Apollo and woven into wreaths to crown victorious generals, athletes and poets in ancient Greece and Rome. In Britain, this tradition still continues in the custom of appointing a Poet Laureate, the nation's official poet whose role it is to compose poems commemorating occasions of national importance. The Roman name for laurel berry, *bacca laureus*, also gives us the terms 'bachelor' in connection with academic honours and *baccalaureat*, the name of the prestigious French academic examination.

MULLEIN

Mullein is traditionally associated with magic. The down of the plant was used by witches to make wicks for the candles they needed for incantations and making spells – hence the herb's other name of 'hag taper'. According to a 17th-century gardening writer, mullein was also known as *Candela regia* because stalks dipped in tallow (rendered animal fat) provided tapers for funerals and other ceremonies.

ORRIS ROOT

Orris root is the root of the Florentine iris, *Iris germanica florentina*. It is an essential ingredient of potpourris and also very important in perfumery. The flower may be seen in the heraldic arms of Florence, and is also thought to be the fleur-de-lis of French heraldry. The word iris itself has mythological connotations, for Iris was the name of the Greek goddess of the rainbow – perhaps an allusion to the many different colours of the flowers.

SWEET CICELY

This herb's botanical name, *Myrrhis odorata*, is thought to refer to the fragrance of its leaves which smell like myrrh.

SOUTHERNWOOD

This herb is said to represent constancy, but it has other associations, too. Its other common name, 'lad's love', refers to the practice of making a paste from the ashes of the plant and then rubbing this on the face to make a beard grow. A powerful insect repellent, it was called *garderobe* (clothes guard) by the French who, like others, placed it in wardrobes to prevent moth infestation.

BORAGE

The Greeks and Romans believed that borage gave courage, and brought happiness and joy.

PENNYROYAL

A species of mint, pennyroyal derives its common name from the old French *pulioll royall*, which referred to a type of thyme. The 'pulegium' in its botanical name, *Mentha pulegium decumbens*, comes from the Latin for 'flea' – *pulex* – which pennyroyal was used to deter.

ROSEMARY

Rosemary is associated with remembrance, and has long had a reputation for improving the memory. Both its common and botanical names – *Rosmarinus* – come from the Latin *ros* and *maris*, which translate as 'dew of the sea'.

THYME

Thyme is said to represent activity and general busyness.

COMFREY

Comfrey's other common name 'knitbone' relates to its traditional use in healing broken bones.

Rosemary

SAGE

Sage represents friendship and esteem. Its botanical name *Salvia* comes from the Latin *salvere*, meaning 'to be in good health', a word which is still found in such modern terms as 'lip salve' referring to a substance's healing properties.

MINT

Mint is associated with wisdom. Its common name and its botanical name, *Mentha*, derive from the Greek myth about a nymph called Minthe, who was changed into a plant by Persephone, queen of the underworld, when she saw her husband, Hades, pursuing the nymph.

FENNEL

In medieval times, fennel was believed to have magic powers and on Midsummer's Eve it was hung above doorways to ward off evil spirits. The herb is also associated with strength and the habit of flattery.

TANSY

The flowers of tansy are reputed to be an excel-lent ingredient in the embalming of corpses, and – appropriately – the herb's name derives from the Greek *athanaton*, meaning 'immortal'.

YARROW

The botanical name for yarrow, *Achillea millefolium*, refers to the tradition that the Greek hero Achilles used the herb to staunch the bleeding from his soldiers' wounds during the Trojan War. Yarrow was also known as *herba militaris*, or military herb.

DILL

Once used in soothing hiccups in infants, dill is said to have acquired its common name from the Anglo-Saxon *dylle* or old Norse *dilla*, meaning to 'lull' or 'soothe'.

VERVAIN

Vervain was regarded both as a cure-all and as a magically potent herb. The Romans called it 'holy herb' and the Druids used it in their rituals.

Tansy

Yarrow

Vervain

Index

Page references in bold indicate directory entry.

D

E

F

G

H

I

K

L

Y

Z

Picture Credits

Elizabeth Whiting & Associates
pp 130-131, 135, 136-137, 139

Food Features
pp 5, 6–7, 11–12, 14, 18–25, 27, 29, 30, 32–33, 35, 36 (top), 37, 39,
41–45, 53, 68-69, 71, 77, 80–84, 86–91, 93–95, 100–103, 105–107, 120,
122, 128, 131,
143–149, 156, 159

Tessa Traeger
pp 13, 47–48, 58–59, 96, 98–99, 108, 133

The Garden Picture Library
pp 8–9, 26, 28, 31, 36 (bottom), 50–52, 54, 56–57, 60, 62–63, 66–67, 72,
73 (top & centre), 74–75, 78, 85

Quarto Publishing
pp 2, 15, 16, 17, 34, 38, 46, 55, 61, 64–65, 70, 73(bottom), 92, 99, 104,
109, 111, 113–119, 121, 123, 125, 127,
132, 141, 150–155